GENERAL REFLECTIONS

GENERAL REFLECTIONS

A Military Man at Large

Michael Gow (signature)

MICHAEL GOW

SCOTS GUARDSMAN

ENLISTED AS A GUARDSMAN 1942
RETIRED AS A GENERAL 1986
HOPEFUL AUTHOR 1987

SOUVENIR PRESS

First published 1991 by Souvenir Press Ltd,
43 Great Russell Street, London WC1B 3PA
and simultaneously in Canada

ISBN 0 285 63047 4

Printed in Great Britain by
WBC Print Ltd, Bridgend, Mid Glamorgan

DEDICATED BY GRACIOUS PERMISSION
TO
HER MAJESTY QUEEN ELIZABETH
THE QUEEN MOTHER

Acknowledgements

I am grateful to the following for allowing me to quote from published material: the Editor of *Punch* for the poem 'The Guards', by Evoe; the Editor of the 'Peterborough' column in the *Daily Telegraph* for permission to use the story about Mrs Susie Ross; Captain Sir Iain Tennant for his permission to reproduce the Alex – Monty letter; and the Salamander Oasis Trust and J.M. Dent & Sons Ltd. for the poems in the Postscript by the late Frank Thompson and my late brother, Roddy Gow.

I thank the following for allowing me to publish photographs and illustrations: Sergeant Harding, Grenadier Guards; the Estate of Sir Osbert Lancaster and John Murray (Publishers) Ltd. for previously published cartoons; John Encombe, Lenare, the Scottish United Services and the Imperial War Museums, the National Galleries of Scotland, the National Museums of Scotland and those who generously allowed me to use material from their private collections.

Finally, I am more grateful than I can say to my friends and relations who as far as I know have not objected to my recollections, and above all to my wife who has, from time to time, viewed my efforts with some misgivings.

Contents

	Acknowledgements	7
	Preface	11
1	The Making of a Man	13
2	Family Anecdotes	25
3	Wifely Remarks	38
4	The Training of a Soldier	47
5	The Guards	58
6	The Scots Guards	61
7	Regimental Headquarters Scots Guards	75
8	Command of the 2nd Battalion Scots Guards	83
9	Commander 4th Guards Brigade	95
10	Commander 4th Armoured Division	102
11	Life in the Ministry	107
12	Scotland and Her Army	118
13	The British Army of the Rhine and NATO's Northern Army Group	126
14	Recollections of 'Abroad'	136
15	Final Appointment	158
16	Military Miscellany	161
17	Tales of the Kirk	173
18	Scottish Vignettes	179
19	Vicissitudes of an Author	191
	Postscript	197

Preface

After my book of anecdotes, called *Jottings in a Gereral's Notebook*, was published, friends and complete strangers asked me to record some more tales and reflections, if there were any left in my faltering memory. By then my wife and I had moved to Scotland and had settled in a street in Edinburgh which the late Sir John Betjeman once described as the prettiest in the United Kingdom. Here I converted what had been a cloakroom into an office, and as I sat at my desk, gazing out over the rooftops and chimneys of the 'New Town', I was very conscious that I had returned to the land of my forebears and to the city whither they moved after being 'out' in the '45 and consequently dispossessed, by the English, of their home in the Highlands.

As thoughts and recollections began to come to mind, I recorded them on a 1932 portable typewriter which a senior aunt had given me. I think she used to take it on trek in Northern Nigeria, carried upon the head of a porter (the machine, not the aunt). This book is meant to give amusement and pleasure to the reader but, like *Jottings*, it contains a postscript in a serious vein because, of course, life comprises fun and sadness, and I would not like anyone to conclude that mine had been one of unending frivolity – a deduction which one media interviewer told me he had made!

I am very honoured to have been allowed to dedicate this book to Queen Elizabeth the Queen Mother. In 1980 I was privileged, as the General Officer Commanding the Army in Scotland, to be responsible for arranging a musical tribute to

Her Majesty in Holyrood Park, and I said then: 'This Tribute comes on this unique occasion from our hearts. I hope this music will show something of our affection and devotion.' I wrote *General Reflections* exactly ten years later on an important anniversary in the life of Her Majesty, who seems eternally young and from whom fun and laughter are never far away. This humble effort marks my own loyalty and affection, and I hope it will give the same enjoyment as did that Musical Tribute.

Anne Street. Edinburgh. From a painting by Claude Jeffrey Dechaume depicting the street some time during the middle of the nineteenth century—it has changed very little since then. The picture shows Lord Jeffreys in his carriage, Lord Cockburn on the far pavement in the centre, and the ghostly figure of the 'Grey Lady' walking on the nearside pavement. *Reproduced by kind permission of Mrs John Maitland Hunt*

1
The Making of a Man

I have recorded here memories of my family and the schools I attended. I read somewhere that you are the person you are as a result of heredity and environment. Although my father died when I was a young child, my brother (who was four years my senior) and I had a happy upbringing in the household of my maternal grandfather. It was very reminiscent of the TV series *Upstairs, Downstairs,* and our nanny, who had brought up my mother, played a very important part in our lives.

MOTHER'S TRAINING

As, I suppose, a preliminary to my entry to Winchester College, whose motto is 'Manners Makyth Man', my mother was keen on teaching me points of etiquette. (I should add that in later life my wife attempted to carry this on: one of her beliefs, for example, upon which she herself had been nurtured, was that when travelling by train it was important to be smartly dressed, and certainly to wear gloves.)

My mother held that when escorting a lady out walking, a gentleman should always be on the outside of the pavement in order to afford protection and, so she said, to have his sword arm free. Considering that I was wearing shorts when I was told this, I could hardly be blamed for thinking it quite irrelevant advice!

I also recall that when I was at prep school, I was invited by a school chum to spend a few days with him at his home in Belgium during the hols. My mother discovered that his parents lived in Brussels. 'That is a capital,' she said. 'Hats are always worn in capitals.' And so a large Homburg hat was bought for me which I was forced to wear on the train journey to Dover, much to my embarrassment and the amusement of fellow-travellers of my own age, and until my mother saw my ship set sail. The moment she was out of sight, I cast it upon the waters.

It was impressed upon me that a gentleman in a lift should immediately remove his hat if a lady entered. On one occasion when I was in Harrods, this situation arose, but when I lifted *my* hat, not only did the ladies who had entered turn round and gaze at me in consternation, but they immediately got out at the next stop. The truth was that I had come from Mr Trumper's hairdressing establishment where I had been persuaded to have my locks sprinkled with some lotion, the scent of which had become trapped beneath my hat until that very moment. It had built up a potency, causing this startling effect when released. I recall

I did not come from a military family. My forebears were artists, musicians and academics, like Dr James Gow, Headmaster of Westminster School 1901–1919, here being saluted by monitors . . .

. . . and his eldest son, Andrew Gow, Scholar of Trinity College, Cambridge, where he returned in 1925, after being a master at Eton for twelve years, as Fellow and Lecturer in Classics and as Tutor from 1929 until 1942, when he became Praelector until his death in 1978.

15

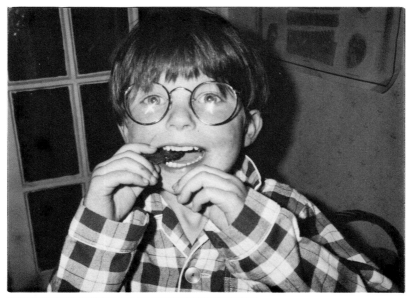

In the family tradition, this grandson may become an academic . . . or a musician. The latter is thought more likely as, aged four, he was heard to say to a departing great-great aunt, 'Well, goodbye, you musical digit!'

that on the label of the bottle Mr Trumper had written, 'particularly efficacious after motoring'.

MOTHER'S ENQUIRY

Before leaving the subject of my late lamented mother, there is one incident worth recording which shows how easily misunderstandings can occur. During a cricket match at Lord's, she happened to meet a friend and enquired after his wife.

'I've lost her,' came the reply.

'Well,' said my mother, 'have you looked behind the pavilion?'

In fact her friend meant that his wife had died.

EARLY SCHOOL EXPERIENCES

At the age of six I went to a pre-preparatory boarding school which, when my brother had been there, had been run by a formidable headmistress called Miss Honeybun, renowned for the corporal punishment which she administered with the back of a hairbrush bearing her initials. The results were known as 'trade-marks' by the recipients, who curiously enough seemed proud of them. The school produced several generals for sure, and no doubt many other men of fame or notoriety. In my time the Head was a man who had served in the Sudan Civil Service and ensured that his pupils were steeped in the history and traditions of the British Empire. Manly sports were high on the curriculum and were considered 'character-building' by my mother who, even earlier in my life, had insisted that every Thursday afternoon I should be taught the art of boxing by a Mr

17

Phipps, a retired bruiser. My opponent was on every occasion the same boy of my own age, whom I 'took on' after tea in the nursery when we always had cream cake. Regularly I made him cry, and he was promptly sick. Mr Phipps then advised against cream cake, which I think was the only reason that the boy came; but looking back on these contests all these years later I am full of admiration for his courage, because he must have known what he was in for!

Mr Phipps's training stood me in good stead at this school, where boxing was compulsory. The end-of-term competition was a major event, and it was generally considered by the punters that a red-headed boy would be the champion; certainly his mother must have had high hopes as she came down to watch her son take on—*me*! I hope that usually I am a modest person, but I must relate that when the first round was announced, I shot out of my corner, delivered a right swinger to red-head's jaw—with an effect that certainly surprised me—felled him to the ground, and caused his deflated mother to remove him from the ring, and the school!

PREP SCHOOL

When I was eight I moved on to a school where my brother was, and subsequently my son and grandsons were to be. I suppose by modern standards Horris Hill would have been considered Spartan: no electricity, one candle per dormitory, and cold baths before a pre-breakfast period in class. These had been filled the evening before, so that it was not uncommon to find ice on the surface—and if you spilt one drop over the side, in you were sent again. Yet not only did we survive but I think we flourished physically and academically. To compose elegiac couplets at the age of

18

J.L. Stow, known as 'Daddy', Headmaster of Horris Hill for many years and a brilliant teacher, cricketer and Head. After my father died, he played a more significant role during the formative years of my life than any other man.

Horris Hill Preparatory School, as it was in the 1930s. The left chimney was struck by lightning, dramatically, during the second course of lunch which was a particularly inedible blancmange of violent colours called 'Ozzy Rainbow'. The top dormitory in the centre swayed alarmingly on windy nights and we were convinced that it was only a matter of time before it collapsed, with us in our beds! *Photo by Salman of Winchester.*

eleven, as we were made to do, was quite an achievement, and I cannot say that I suffered at all from the disciplines that were imposed on us all during those formative years.

The masters were, almost without exception, outstanding 'personalities', and I regret that I never met A.J. Evans, the founder of the school, about whom I was once told the following tale:

A boy had written to his father, listing a number of complaints on every aspect of Horris Hill, and as a result the father came down in a fury to see Evans. He was listened to by the Headmaster with patience and courtesy, and when at last the diatribe ended, Evans refuted each with such effect that the father apologised profusely, saying, 'Mr Evans, I wish to apologise. Clearly I have been misled. I now have no intention of removing my boy from your excellent school.' To which Evans replied, 'How wrong you are. Your son is outside; his trunk is packed, and you will take him away at once!'

WINCHESTER COLLEGE

For a junior 'man', as boys at Winchester are called, a major feature of life was fagging (or being 'in sweat'). Amongst the many menial tasks that came my way was preparation of the prefects' tea every Sunday before evening chapel. I was in charge of the sandwiches, which had to be wafer-thin, and with the crust removed—or woe betide! Having done that, I was then on duty at the front door to receive guests, who naturally were male, and escort them up to the sanctum. (For any man to be seen with a member of the opposite sex was considered then very bad form, and even sisters were frowned upon.)

One Sunday I was on the look-out for the Bishop of Winchester who had been invited, but I was suddenly taken short and asked a friend to hold the fort for a minute or two.

On my return, much to my annoyance, I found that my friend had disappeared, and I prayed that all was well as time was marching on. I peered down the street, and to my relief espied a gaitered figure coming along. I sprang forward and greeted him: 'Good afternoon, sir, very pleased to see you. Step this way.' He started to speak but I interrupted, 'No need to apologise as you aren't late. Just follow me,' and I took him rapidly along. I flung open the sanctum door and in a loud voice announced, 'The Bishop of Winchester.' As I said these words I saw, to my utter astonishment, another bishop sitting there. Heavens! It was the Bishop of Winchester, whom my friend had taken up. I had intercepted the Bishop of Southampton who happened by chance to be passing!

The aftermath of my error was somewhat painful.

REBELLION!

From time to time Winchester College has been stricken by revolts, one of which, many years ago, resulted in the military being summoned to the aid of the school authorities. Then there was the Great Tunding Scandal in the last century ('tunding' being the 'notions' word for beating). As one of the editors of the school magazine, I wrote a racy article about it which was censored as being on too 'delicate' a subject. but when I was the Senior Prefect of my House in 1942, quite a gratifying demonstration of revolt erupted, involving arson and the placing of a (harmless) device in the Headmaster's car. I also seem to remember that at about the same time a junior master was reported as having been arrested by the city police for drunkenness and high jinks in the High Street, which all added to the fun.

I was something of a confidant of the Headmaster, the Reverend Spencer Leeson, who gave me private tuition in constitutional history and public instruction in the classics.

'School' at Winchester College, where the Headmaster intended to address the riotous Wykehamists, provided that it was still standing.

As the situation hotted up, he sent for me for advice as to what he should do.

'Well, sir, I would recommend that you might address the whole school in "School"'—'School' being an impressive hall built by or in the style of Wren.

I clearly recall his comment: 'But, Gow, when I get there, School may not be standing!'

World War II was raging at that time and the country was bracing itself for the reception of bomber raids, but *our* problems seemed then much more important and much more exciting. How it all ended, I cannot now remember, but the fabric of Winchester college survived these vicissitudes.

A LESSON IN CHAPEL

In my time there was no nonsense about voluntary chapel attendance. We went there to worship daily, and twice on Sunday, and I always thought that our founder, William of Wykeham, would have strongly disapproved of anything else. These services, during which the singing, especially of the choir (of which I was a member as treble, alto, tenor (and bass), was beautiful, left a lasting mark on me. Prefects read the lessons, and my only brush with the Headmaster was over my rendering of a passage from the Book of Job. Job always struck me as a pretty gloomy fellow, always moaning on about his illnesses, and I was reading a conversation between him and the Almighty. In order to make it 'come alive' I gave Job what seemed to me an appropriate voice while the Almighty, who knew all, spoke cheerfully and with confidence. Later I was sent for by the Headmaster, who was accompanied by at least one chaplain, and reprimanded. I suppose they had a point.

But school chaplains *then* had clear religious duties as well as being dons. Things changed later, and I met a school cleric who told me that he was a 'counsellor'. This was a new one on me, and he explained that the men could come and seek his advice on any problem.

'Why can't they go to their housemasters like we used to do?' I asked.

'Oh no,' came the reply, 'that would never do. The house dons have powers of discipline, you see. For example, I had a chap in here the other day; he was about to have a rather painful interview with his house don, and he said to me, "Sir, do you think it would be good tactics and helpful to my cause if at this moment in the interview I suddenly burst into tears?"'

I was amazed, and certainly did not do that when *I* attended upon the Head!

A HEADMASTER'S ADDRESS

Having delivered what he thought to be an especially effective address in chapel, a headmaster was gratified to be told by the Head of School afterwards that his message had come across like the 'Peace of God'. Much pleased, the Head unwisely asked him to elaborate. 'Well, sir,' he replied, 'I can safely say that as far as the school was concerned, yours passed all our understanding!'

2
Family Anecdotes

Since I got married, my family has been the most important factor in my life, although a soldier sometimes finds a sharp conflict between his military and domestic inclinations and responsibilities. This book would be incomplete without my recording a few memories and anecdotes.

A PROPOSAL OF MARRIAGE

I remember my brother once telling me that a certain Warden of Winchester College had been turned down when he made his marriage proposal. The reason was that, having seated his Intended upon a garden bench in surroundings which he judged to be appropriately romantic, he had taken from his pocket a handkerchief which he carefully placed upon the ground before he knelt. This so shocked the lady in question that, when he asked, she declined!

I was determined to avoid this sort of mistake. I had saved up £160 from my army pay, which allowed me to take my hoped-for wife to dinner and to a night-club in London about a dozen times, to 'soften her up', as it were, before the Great Occasion—the Guards Boat Club Ball. (Sadly, this club on the Thames at Maidenhead is long since gone, and the ball, which was a major event in the social calendar before and, for a short time, after the War, is but a distant memory.) I had planned everything with care and had strategically placed a punt by the jetty in advance. As we approached the craft I subconsciously noticed movement in the adjoining shrubbery, but thought nothing of it. I gallantly handed my Intended into the boat and cast off. Almost at once I felt moisture in my shoes, and the water rose rapidly. We were sinking! It was a miracle that we made the shore and were able to get out, as the punt filled to the gunwales.

Those who had been lurking in the bushes and who, needless to say, were fellow-officers in the Scots Guards, had eased out the bung, and as a result my future wife spent the rest of the ball crouched over a brazier, drying off in a cloud of steam. It was a miracle that, unlike the Warden's, my proposal was accepted, but for a long time she was not very enthusiastic about the military!

My future wife in the dress she was wearing for the romantic but disastrous evening at the Guards Boat Club Ball.

HONEYMOON

We were married fairly soon after the War, when peacetime conditions had certainly not yet been restored. One of my wife's grandfathers was a director of a leading travel agency, and when I approached him about our honeymoon he advised me to consult a member of the staff who seemed to me not only ancient and well past retirement age but also somewhat out of touch with the times. Anyway, he booked us into an hotel in Paris which he personally recalled from pre-1914 days and warmly recommended. On arrival, however, we found that it had dramatically sunk to *troisième classe*, but at least we were in romantic Paris at the start of our honeymoon.

The first day was occupied visiting a Monsieur Socrate who, on a previous visit that my wife had paid with her father, had exchanged a smart lady's hat for one of the latter's suits. I felt duty-bound to do the same, and thus it was that my wife was able later to appear at the annual Eton and Winchester cricket match wearing what looked to me like a bowl of fruit salad on her head.

During my courting days I had told her of my fluent mastery of the French language, so perhaps it was understandable that when she found that there were no bath towels she asked me to ring up the manager and demand some. I tried to explain that France was still suffering from the economic aftermath of war and occupation, but she would have none of it. I went into the bathroom to find out from my pocket dictionary the French words, but was briskly asked what I was doing and to hurry up. So I rang Reception and asked, only to be told to go out of the front door of the hotel and turn left, and I would find them three hundred metres further down on the right. These, I discovered, were directions to the Turkish Baths!

This was a set-back, not improved when my wife said she would like to go to a dashing night-club. I consulted

Reception, then off we set on foot for what seemed a long time, with me frequently consulting the map. (This is where I thought my military experience would pay off!) Disaster, however, struck again when we arrived at the address, which was a disused warehouse.

When things go badly wrong, I am usually cheerful because it is only a matter of time before there is a turn-up. How wrong I was! The next blow fell when we boarded the train for Switzerland, only to find that it had no restaurant car, and we had had no dinner—nor had we taken any food with us. We arrived the next morning at Berne, very hungry, and the banks had not opened so I had no money! And to cap it all we had thought our destination was Lugano, only to find that it was Locarno!

When we finally left for home, we spent a great deal of money buying things that we thought were unprocurable in England (like two doz. bananas), and had difficulty crossing the frontier into France as the customs officials of both countries asked to see our export/import licences. When eventually we did arrive back, we were hardly on speaking terms, not least when we found that we could have bought in England most of the things with which we were burdened.

I rather selfishly thought it the last straw that, as we climbed out of the train at Victoria Station—who should be waiting for us? The mother-in-law! (I should, however, add that the latter was a woman for whom I later had the greatest respect and affection.)

Believe it or not—after such an inauspicious start—my wife and I have been happily married for all these years!

THE MOTHER-IN-LAW

She was a very remarkable woman, daughter of Jack Seely, Lord Mottistone, who himself was an equally singular man: a soldier who did not know what fear was (and it was said, rather unkindly, that in World War I, when he commanded the Canadian Cavalry Brigade and had recommended his orderly for the VC, the citation included the words, 'He never left my side'). He was a member of the House of Commons, had held office as Secretary of State for War, had fought with a Yeomanry Cavalry regiment in the South African War and had practised at the Bar. His daughter, my mother-in-law, disapproved of showing emotion of any sort in public; once, when I said to her that I did not suppose she would like a sweet, to my surprise she replied that she would—but it was important to eat it sitting bolt upright.

My wife-to-be in South America before the War with her parents, younger sister, brother and friends.

She had, at one time, a fixation against Teddy Boys, and when living in London always put a bucket of water by her open bedroom window to pour on the heads of any below whom she thought noisy. One night there *was* an animated conversation in the street, and she tipped the bucket over the offenders. All hell was then let loose, there was banging on the front door, and her husband, who was known in the family as 'Squire', only just intercepted the Spanish *au pair*, who had been aroused by the clamour and was about to let them in.

When she moved to a house in Chester Square, somehow the removal men managed to get into the basement a very large piano, which my small son used to play. Quite often a crowd would collect on the pavement and gaze down on him, admiring the music of this infant prodigy. Little did they know that he was actually playing a pianola! When the family moved yet again, my mother-in-law no longer wanted this instrument and asked if I could think of anyone who might like it. I said that I knew the sergeants' mess of the Scots Guards at Wellington Barracks would be delighted, and its removal was set in train. Unfortunately, however, it was found to be impossible to get it out of the basement in one piece, and so it was dismantled.

There was at one time a popular TV programme called *Candid Camera*, which produced hilarious situations such as a driver asking the attendant at a petrol filling station to check his engine oil, only to discover, when the bonnet was lifted, that there was no engine there at all. And so it was that, when the removal men arrived at the barracks, one of them went into the sergeants' mess, which was occupied only by the barman. 'I've brought a grand piano for you, mate,' he said, holding merely the keyboard, and it was very difficult indeed to persuade the Scots Guards that it was a bona fide instrument and intended as a gift!

TRYING TO MAKE BOTH ENDS MEET

We were married so young that the Army refused to acknowledge our marital status, with the result that we had no quarter allotted to us and no marriage allowance until I was aged 25, and before that we had had two children. As a result we were somewhat financially embarrassed, and we decided that the solution was to 'moonlight'; but this would have to be done with secrecy, as it would incur the gravest displeasure of the authorities in Horse Guards and Headquarters Scots Guards if it became known.

Our plan was to form an extremely efficient but expensive catering organisation: my wife would be the cook and I the butler, and as a team we would guarantee to any employer an evening's entertainment of the highest standard. So seriously did we consider this enterprise that I went to a well known London dress hire firm to be kitted out. I can see myself now in the mirror of the fitting-room, wearing a yellow and black striped waistcoat and a swallow-tail coat with large gold buttons. I asked to reserve this outfit for two days a week.

On my return home I found, however, that my wife had had second thoughts. She had worked out that although we would be very expensive, albeit extremely efficient, to hire, by the time we had bought the food and drink, hired taxis to and fro and engaged a baby-sitter, we would have to be so costly that no one could possibly afford our invaluable services. I was very disappointed; I could just see myself throwing open the door and announcing, 'Dinner is served, Your Grace'—or, in my wilder flights of imagination, 'Dinner is served, Your Royal Highness'!

HELP FROM AN UNCLE

When we got married, my wife's youngest sister, Jenny, was a babe in arms. Some years later I found her as a schoolgirl aged about seven, struggling one evening with her 'prep'. It was arithmetic, and as she was clearly in difficulties, I gallantly offered my assistance. 'I'll have to say that it wasn't all my own work,' she said, so she wrote at the bottom, 'Helped by Major Gow'.

The next time I saw her, I asked how she had got on. 'Not too hot,' she replied. 'We only got 4 out of 12 right, and the teacher said, "Next time, Jenny, try to get someone more reliable to help you"!'

My Father-in-law, Captain Mason Scott RN, MFH, known *en famille* as 'Squire', blows 'Gone Away' on the departure of his youngest daughter after her wedding. *Photo: John Encombe.*

PHYSICAL DAMAGE

Next time you see my brother-in-law Brough Scott, the racing commentator, on the 'box', have a look at his arms, because when he was a small boy I used to swing him round, briskly and off the ground, by holding on to them.

His mother used to reprimand me. 'Don't do that! You'll make him deformed!' I pictured her taking him to the health clinic and saying, 'Doctor, what's wrong with Brough? He's not like the other boys. He doesn't have to bend down to do up his shoe laces!'

Perhaps I unwittingly contributed to his racing style and it was this that enabled him to become the leading amateur jockey!

Brough Scott in 1968, while an undergraduate at Oxford where he read history. Despite eighty rides during a season, he still got his degree. He gave up riding as an amateur and professional in 1971. *Photo: John Encombe.*

THE IMPORTANCE OF AN ADDRESS

I was in an appointment at the Guards Depot, which at that time was at Caterham, when one day my son, who was at Winchester College, asked me, 'How much longer do you think it will be before you are posted from here?'

I asked him why he wanted to know, and his reply was interesting: 'Now don't think I'm a snob, but it is a bit embarrassing. The school list gives all the addresses of the men in the school; the chap above me lives in a castle in Scotland and the one below in a manor house in Gloucestershire, and there in between is me: "Gow, R.C. (G House). 150 Foxon Lane, Caterham, Surrey". It rather lets the side down, don't you think?'

INITIATIVE

Some years ago, my eyes fell upon a newspaper cutting which read as follows: 'TUTOR: ex-Winchester student, awaiting entry to Trinity, Cambridge, seeks post in family abroad as English tutor from end of March. Write box . . . *The Times'*.

'Just look at this,' I exclaimed to my son. 'Here's someone just like you! Why don't you show a bit of initiative?'

'Oh, I have,' he replied. 'That's my advert, and she has agreed to my terms.'

I was mystified and asked him to explain.

'Well, you kept telling me to do something positive and I have! I put that advert in, and a charming aristocratic Spanish lady replied, asking me to send further particulars, which I did.'

'But what about these "terms" of yours?'

'I told her that I should expect a first-class return air ticket, a room of my own as a study, a bedroom suite, the services of a personal valet, naturally to be treated as one of the family, have exclusive use of a car, teach English for not more than two hours a day, and be paid a good salary.'

'You must be mad,' I exclaimed. 'She'll never agree!'

'Oh yes indeed she will, and what's more, she has. I'm off next week. Funny! I thought I'd told you.'

THE PSYCHOLOGY OF A TEST

My wife's driving licence had expired, and although she had driven for several years in Germany and thereafter on the continent, and with a visitor's licence in the United Kingdom, the inevitable happened, and she was instructed to report for a test.

'Your Mother may have a bit of difficulty in passing,' I warned the family. 'We must give her maximum support.'

Accordingly, we all accompanied her to the town where she was to be put through her paces. En route, I said to her, 'Don't forget. You may have to do a three-point turn.'

'Three-point turn!' she exclaimed. 'Whatever's that?'

So we found a secluded stretch of road for her to practise, but the best she achieved was a twelve-pointer, and we had to stop as she would have been late for the test.

We assembled on the pavement after she had reported in, and she sat, somewhat tensed behind the wheel, waiting for the tester to appear.

'Here he comes,' declared one of the children.

'Oh good,' I said. 'Look! He's got my letter on his millboard.'

This document was psychologically vital; in it I had explained that I was a major in a Scots Guards battalion of the Strategic Reserve. I painted a vivid picture of us being on permanent standby to fly immediately to any trouble spot in the world. (I may even have added that my combat kit was permanently ready at home for me to spring into, and that I kept my gas mask by my bed.) The point was that *when*, rather than *if*, I went, it was desperately important that this mother of five should be able to drive, otherwise all, domestically, would be lost. As he embarked, and my wife gingerly drove off, we stood there waving. 'Good luck, Mum. We're sure you'll be OK and pass easily,' we shouted, and then repaired to the nearby Wimpy Bar for chips, waiting with apprehension and peering out nervously.

'Here she is!' shouted one of our observers; and we saw her, very red in the face, in earnest discussion with the tester. After what seemed ages, he handed her a paper and disappeared whence he had come.

Out we all went and piled into the car. 'Well? What happened?' she was asked, and mopping her fevered brow she announced that she had passed.

'Hurrah!' shouted the kids.

'Amazing,' I murmured. 'Any problems?'

'Not really,' she replied. 'It was a bit embarrassing when I went up a one-way street the wrong way, and then didn't notice that the traffic lights were red. But he was such a nice young man. He said I reminded him of his mother, and he realised that I had a problem—(you)—which he was taking into consideration.'

So there is nothing like a moving letter to achieve results.

CHARISMA

'I do wish,' I once remarked, 'that I were like one of those chaps you sometimes read about in books.'

'Whatever are you talking about?' I was asked.

'Oh, you know. The scene is a fashionable party. The room is full of people of distinction—the Prime Minister, let us say, a sprinkling of the Diplomatic Corps, tycoons of industry and commerce, the international jet set . . . Then the door opens and HE comes in. Such is the charisma of his personality that instinctively all conversation stops; all eyes are riveted upon him in admiration . . . You know the sort of thing I mean.'

'Well, that would never happen to you,' one of the family commented, 'unless, that is, you had forgotten to put your trousers on!'

3
Wifely Remarks

Below I reveal some of the more remarkable facets of my wife to whom I have been married for nearly 45 years and with whose help I have mustered five children and nine grandchildren.

A HOTEL CONVERSATION

We happened to be staying in a hotel where the late Sir Adrian and Lady Boult were fellow-guests. I overheard the following snippet of conversation between the two ladies:

Music off
Lady Boult: 'Ah! Bach!'
My wife: 'Oh I don't think so. Dogs aren't allowed in here, you know!'
(Recent extract from the *Ely Standard*: 'Cambridgeshire Village Colleges Choral Society: Bark, St John Passion. Ely Cathedral'.)

ENTRY TO EDINBURGH CASTLE

When I was the Governor of Her Majesty's Castle, we lived in the Governor's apartments from after Hogmanay till the end of March. When visitors and tourists had departed, the gates were closed and placed under the control of a military guard.

One evening it was raining hard when my wife arrived back from shopping. Much encumbered with parcels and a dog, and wearing a sodden head-scarf and mackintosh, she knocked on the massive gate. A trap slid back and a face peered out. The subsequent conversation went something like this:

Sentry: 'Hello, what do you want?'
Wife: 'Please let me in. I'm the wife of the Governor.'
S: Don't give me that. If you're the Governor's wifey, I'm the Queen of Sheba.'
W: 'I know that governors' wives shouldn't look like me, and normally I shouldn't be looking like this,

but you see I've been out shopping and it's very wet and I just want to get in.'

S: 'Where's your identity card?'

W: 'I'm afraid I haven't got one.'

S: 'How do I know you're not a terrorist? Look at those bags—full of bombs nae doot.'

W: 'You can look inside and see. I've just got the Governor's supper and he'll be waiting for it.'

S: 'Well, doggies aren't allowed in here anyways.'

W: (*A brain-wave*) 'That is the Governor's dog. It says so on his collar. Just look!'

Grudgingly the sentry did so, and read the words: 'Frodo. Governor. Edinburgh Castle'.

And that's how my wife managed to get home!

The guarded entrance to Edinburgh Castle through which my wife found it difficult to pass.

A COMMENT ON THE INTERNATIONAL SITUATION

Once when we happened to find ourselves in the company of one of our most important national leaders and spouse, the latter said to my wife, 'Don't you think what's happening in Eastern Europe is very exciting?' My wife agreed. 'And what about Berlin, which you must know well?' And my wife agreed that that too was very exciting. 'And the Wall! You must have been through Checkpoint Charlie many times, and you must be amazed that the wall is coming down? '

To this my wife's comment was rather singular: 'I do hope that they are careful when they knock it down; someone could be badly hurt if a brick fell on their head!'

This comment on the international situation was received with some astonishment, and I thought that an intervention might be prudent. 'Actually, if you think about it, my wife may well be right,' I remarked. 'If a West Berliner dropped a brick on the head of a passing Russian general and killed or disabled him, that's how World War III could be started'—and our companion had to agree to that possibility, though, I thought, with some reluctance!

THE SALE OF A HOUSE

The sale of our house in the south before we moved to Scotland was somewhat fraught. To start with, during an interview for a series in a national Sunday paper's supplement called 'A Room of My Own' (which, in fact, wasn't mine at all but that of my wife, in which, much to her fury, most of her belongings and ornaments had been replaced by mine in order to give some credence to the article), I was reported as having said, somewhat rashly, 'Of course, only a maniac would buy a house like this', referring to my height and the lowness of the ceilings.

The house in England which we sold, with the 'signalling station' hill beyond.

In order to cope expeditiously with the stream of potential buyers when we put it on the market, we developed a 'drill'. I gave them a general briefing about the antiquity and historical importance of the property, and showed them the 'policies' before handing over to my wife, who dealt with the interior. I recall saying to one group, 'Now that hill there is extremely interesting. Not only is it the site of an ancient fort, but in Nelson's time it was a signalling station and . . . '

Whereupon the 'group leader' interjected, '. . . on a clear day a message could be transmitted from the Admiralty to Portsmouth in twenty minutes.'

'However did you know that?' I asked. 'Do you come from these parts?'

'No,' was the reply. 'You told me all that when I came here yesterday!'

After a while I had to ban my wife from speaking at all. All her life she had been very keen on honesty, but now, I felt, she was going too far. '. . . As you can see, the central heating is pretty poor and only gives background warmth. And if the wind is in the north, my word it really is cold. The wind and draughts come in through all the nooks and crannies. We had that slow-burning wood stove put in recently—at vast expense. Pretty good waste of time, if you ask me . . . and another thing. I'll tell you about the hot water system. With a family of any size at all you've got to be jolly careful . . .'

The sale price that we were aiming for, and that I assumed should be the maximum, seemed to be a matter of some indifference to her. 'I don't like that lot,' she would say; or, 'Nice people, but I don't think that young wife would be happy here. Not used to the country, I can see.'

So at last we sold, probably under price, to a family whom my wife considered most likely to be happy in our old home—and I must be honest: I think she was right!

A QUESTION OF CONVENIENCE

My wife was a little doubtful about our intended move to Edinburgh; she really favoured a croft in Wester Ross at the back of beyond. So she decided that we would take a house for a month in a street where we might possibly settle. The plan was that if she felt the ambiance to be genial, she would then establish 'contacts' who would alert her whenever a house came on the market—an event which, we were told, was rare. An added complication was that she said she could only live on one side of the street and between two particular numbers, which led me to suggest that she should visit an oculist as she must be suffering from tunnel vision. Curiously enough, in the event her master-plan worked; her contacts got in touch, and she bought the precise house that she had had in mind!

Before that moment, however, she became very nearly *persona non grata* in that select street: during our reconnaissance she had asked me if we intended any entertaining, and I had said that of course we would in order to establish these vital 'contacts' about whom she kept talking, and to demonstrate to our future neighbours what charming and cultured people we were.

'Well, the "facilities" are quite inadequate,' she said. 'There's only one cloakroom and that's upstairs. I'll have to make some special arrangements.'

One day I heard her on the telephone, talking to Glasgow. 'Right—£300 for two weeks?' she was saying . . .

'Wait a minute,' I interjected. 'Just let me talk to this fellow,' and I seized the apparatus. '£300 for two weeks? That's absolutely ridiculous!'

But the voice at the other end replied, 'Well, sir, it is a 40-seater!'

Had I not put a stopper on it, the convenience would have occupied several 'Residents Only' parking spaces, and we would never have been accepted as desirable neighbours, however hard we had tried to be charming and cultured.

A MATTER OF IDENTITY

I witnessed a curious incident one day, which I reported to my wife. One of the most interesting and popular exhibits in the Scottish United Services Museum in Edinburgh Castle is a stuffed figure of the 'Dog Bob', who was on the strength of the Scots Fusilier Guards, later renamed the Scots Guards, during the Crimean War. (He had been present at all the battles and had been awarded a special regimental medal for bravery. All this is described in detail in a framed, written explanation which hangs beside his show case.) One day a lady came in to the museum with a child, and they stood admiring Bob. She read out the account of his history to the child, and every time she came to the word 'dog' she said 'cat'.

The Dog Bob, hero of the Crimean War.
Photo: National Museums of Scotland.

I was reminded of this some time later when we became members of a local select and beautiful garden, into which key-holders were allowed by the rules to take no more than two dogs. We had (and have) three: two Border terriers and a Peke called Poppy.

'What are you going to do?' I asked my wife.

'No problem,' she replied. 'If asked, I shall merely say that Poppy is a cat.'

And that is what she does!

A MATTER OF INTERPRETATION

Anyone having a conversation with my wife has either to have his or her wits sharp or to be psychic, as she always assumes that others know what she has in her mind. Thus, in a club in Edinburgh she suddenly remarked, 'I've just seen some old friends going into the Smoking-Room.'

'Oh, who are they?'

'You know who I mean—the, er, um . . . the Kyles of Lochalsh.'

'You don't mean that at all! They're the Camerons of Lochiel!'

'There you are', she exclaimed. 'You knew exactly who I meant!'

A GRACE FOR OUR NEW HOME

O Lord who blessed the loaves and fishes
Look down upon these sumptuous dishes.
Be gracious to the House of Gow
And bless this food before us now. Amen.

4

The Training of a Soldier

My interest in the military began when I was about six or seven. My brother and I started to collect lead soldiers, which we laid out on a special table at the start of each holiday and packed away with great care at the end, as a result of which they were kept in pristine condition. We had nearly 2,000 of them at, I think, one shilling and sixpence per box, and I saw a similar box on sale in London recently for well over £150. Like a fool I gave them all away during the War!

My grandfather, who was in no sense a military man, used to inspect them, and I remember him saying on one of these occasions, 'Whom do I observe at the head of the column?', to which we replied, 'An officer of the Guards.'

'Officer of the Guards!' he exclaimed. 'That will never do! Put an officer of the Royal Engineers up front. I'm told that is the custom, as the leader must have brains!'

At Horris Hill all the boys were trained by a retired sergeant of Boer War vintage, who was also the groundsman, in the drill to which he had been accustomed. I am not sure that we 'formed square to receive cavalry', but we might well have done.

THE HOME GUARD

My military life really began in the Home Guard. As a result of the hilarious TV serial 'Dad's Army' this Force has become something of a joke, but when it was formed it was considered very seriously. In his diaries the late Richard Meinertzhagen recalled that in 1940 he was Home Guard Commander responsible for the defence of Westminster, including Downing Street. His troops were recruited from clubland, the British Museum and the Stock Exchange, and one platoon (improbably, one would think) included a duke and ten earls. It may well have been this platoon whose commander enlisted help in training from the Irish Guards, who sent a drill sergeant to put them through their paces.

'Well, I'm afraid you'll never make a soldier,' said this Mick to a senior citizen in the ranks, who had great difficulty in sloping arms.

'Oh I don't know,' came the reply. 'I commanded a Corps in the last war!'

'And please remember, Sir Horace, that your distinctions in civil life mean little or nothing to us in the Auxiliary Fire Brigade. Cartoon by Osbert Lancaster. *Reproduced by permission of the Estate of Sir Osbert Lancaster and John Murray (Publishers) Ltd*

THE WINCHESTER COLLEGE PLATOON

Looking back on my time at Winchester during the War, what was remarkable was that life went on as it always had: there seemed to be no change in the pattern of our lives. The Eton and Winchester match was played as usual, the school tuck-shop seemed to be immune to the restrictions of rationing, and so on. It is true that occasionally when the air raid sirens went off at night we moved into the basements, and we carried our gas masks, but any excessive concern for the War was discouraged. A notice was put up in 1940 asking for volunteers to put 'scrim' on to camouflage nets, a task to which I felt a patriotic duty to contribute, but my efforts were ill received by my 'Div Don' (or form master), who told me that by doing so I had missed a period on Lucretius which was far more important.

The College did, however, raise a platoon of the Home Guard under the command of a splendid and popular don who also ran the Officer Training Corps, later renamed the 'Junior Training Corps' because it was considered wrong, socially or politically, by left-wing elements in Parliament that we should assume that we would become, in due course, officers. I was appointed the Platoon Sergeant, and in the ranks as privates were my own housemaster, a veteran of World War I, and a don who became Lord James of Rusholme and High Master of Manchester Grammar School. I hoped that both would react instantly to the whiplash of my sharp commands. We were all keen, and I have often wondered how we would have acquitted ourselves had Hitler's invasion taken place. At any rate years later, when on an official visit to Bulgaria and Yugoslavia, I impressed the local military top brass, who kept talking about the great achievements of their partisans, by saying that I too had been trained as a partisan, and so we were 'brothers in arms'. This went down well!

PSYCHOLOGICAL SET-BACKS?

By all accounts my personality should have been permanently scarred. It all started when I was about 13 and was taken by my mother to meet a friend of hers in Edinburgh, where we lived. 'I am so very pleased to see you,' the friend said to me. 'I hear that you are at school at Winchester so you must be very clever.' Whereupon my mother replied, 'Oh no, *this* isn't the clever one. You mean his brother—*this* one didn't get a scholarship.' I was cut to the quick, and later told her that she had delivered a serious blow to my ego and that I should never forget what she had said—and I never have!

When I went to the Guards Depot, Caterham (alias 'Little Sparta') as 2701193 Recruit Gow J., Scots Guards, I was one of the lowest of the low, or so we were told on arrival. The shock to the system was severe. On the very first morning the recruit standing at the next basin to mine in the 'ablutions' attempted suicide with a cut-throat razor, which was an indicator to me that the place was unlikely to be in the holiday camp category.

An early and of course compulsory visit to the barber's shop, however, temporarily reassured me. 'Good morning,' said the corporal in charge. 'Just sit here please. And how would we like our hair cut this morning? A little trim at the back, and I think, perhaps, if you agree, it might be thinned a trifle?'

'Oh yes, please,' I replied unwittingly.

'What do you mean, 'Yes please', you horrible scruffy individual! And you will sit to attention and call me "Corporal". You're not in the male chorus of the Follies Bergeries now!' he shouted; and out came the electric clippers, with predictable results!

And later, on the barrack square: 'Call yourself a Scots Guardsman? If His Majesty the King could see you, he'd abdicate! Do you know what *you* look like? I'll tell you: you look to me very much like a bag of manure tied up with pink string!'

Unless one maintained a sense of humour in life—and especially at the Guards Depot—one was doomed.

A MILITARY SET-BACK

I was immensely proud when I successfully passed out from the Depot at the end of the recruits' course, and even more relieved actually to be allowed out of the gate past the watchful and critical eye of the Sergeant of the Guard. Several times in the past I had been turned back for some error of dress or general deportment. 'His Majesty's Guards don't stand about at street corners with a tuppenny bag of crisps in their hand chatting up the birds, y'know . . . and that's just what you look to me as if you might be going to do,' I was told at one attempt. This time, however, I made it and felt ten foot tall, with the Scots Guards flash on the shoulders of my battledress jacket for all the world to see—and admire.

One Wednesday at Pirbright, where the next stage of training took place, I was marched before the Commanding Officer and appointed a Lance Corporal. At once I went to the tailor's shop and had the stripes sewn on my sleeve; I could almost feel them burning into my flesh! To be able to enter the corporals' mess was a privilege far greater to me than being elected, later in life, to a grand and select London club.

Pride, however, comes before a fall: the following day I was put in charge of a fatigue party to clean out the NAAFI (or canteen). It was 1000 hours. The place was inspected at 1030 and found to be in 'bad order', and at 1200 I appeared before the Commanding Officer and was demoted for inefficiency.

I've often wondered what might have happened to me if the NAAFI had been found in *good* order; I might have ended up as a regimental sergeant major (alias God).

THE ROYAL MILITARY ACADEMY SANDHURST

In my time the Academy was called 100 Officer Cadet Training Unit (Royal Armoured Corps), and anyone aspiring to a commission in regiments equipped with tanks or armoured cars had to endure a six-month course there. Looking back on it now, it was a sort of madhouse, and I did not enjoy it. There were three cadets to a room in which were one bed, which had always been there, and a double-tier bunk with straw-filled palliasses. Every third week one slept in the bed, in comparative comfort, but life was not easy. Some found it difficult to adjust: I am told that once in 1940 a sergeant major was calling the roll of his cadets who stood on parade, coming to attention when their names were shouted out.

'Officer Cadet Lord Richard Percy!'

Up went a window. 'Here; I'll be down in a tick!'

This was *not* well received.

Almost my only personal recollection of the place was the comment of a cavalry officer instructor, hot-foot from the Western Desert, who told us, 'Y'know, the waiters in Shepherd's Hotel were tewwibly off-hand when Wommel was advancing on Caiwo.' He was meant to be teaching us how to use a sun compass, about which he knew nothing. 'Don't get too fussed. Your twoop sar'nt will know what to do. They're wather twicky.'

However, we *were* taught a great deal about the intricacies of tank engines that we would never see and guns that we would never fire, though precious little, as far as I can recall, about how to command a troop of tanks which, presumably, was why we were there.

The Adjutant shows off his horsemanship, riding up the steps of the Old College at the end of the Sovereign's Parade.

THE ADJUTANT'S WIFE

Writing of Sandhurst reminds me that many years later, when talking to a young officer in Germany, I asked him what year he had been at the Academy. When he told me, I said that he must have known my son-in-law, the Adjutant. Yes, he had. And so, I added, he must also have met the Adjutant's wife, my eldest daughter.

The Adjutant's wife.
Photo: Lenare

'Well,' came the reply, 'not exactly.'

'What do you mean?' I asked, somewhat mystified.

'Well my friends and I used to get to chapel early . . .'

'Yes?'

'Well, sir, if you really want to know, we got there early in order to get good seats so that we could gaze at the Adjutant's wife!'

I was, of course unaware of this when occasionally I accompanied her to services, during one of which the chaplain preached a remarkable sermon on the dangers of orgies—and I was told that the evening before he had been dining in the Commandant's house!

THE ACADEMY SERGEANT MAJOR

The warrant officer who holds this appointment is always a Guardsman—in my time a Grenadier called 'Bosom Brand' because of his shape—and the most senior in the military hierarchy of outstanding men. It would be difficult to begin to assess the influence that Academy Sergeant Majors have had on the thousands of cadets, British and overseas, who have passed through Sandhurst. ('You, sir, are the idlest king I have ever come across,' was the comment made on one royal cadet from abroad.)

When my son-in-law was appointed Adjutant, he and his family lived on the campus at Lake House (sometimes called 'Pond Cottage'). One day I thought I would visit them, and arrived by car in fog. I was told that they were all down at Victory College where the cadets were practising for a parade at Buckingham Palace at which the Queen was to present a new Sovereign's Banner. So off I went, found the family, and settled down to watch the proceedings in drifting mist.

'Right, gentlemen,' announced one of the College Sergeant Majors. 'You are now standing in the forecourt of Buckingham Palace on this great occasion. Look to the left. Who do you see? You *think* you see the Academy Sergeant Major, but you are wrong. For the purposes of this rehearsal that is *not* the Sergeant Mayor. THAT is—er—none other than—uh—Her *Majesty THE QUEEN!*'

They were then called to attention, and Sergeant Major Huggins, Grenadier Guards, advanced, pace stick under his arm but in all other respects doing his best with dignity to represent the Sovereign. Unfortunately (or so I thought), the 'Queen' rather spoilt the image by suddenly stopping and shouting out, 'Sergeant Major, take the name of the officer cadet, second from the left in the rear rank. Moving about on parade!'

PHYSICAL FITNESS

Hardly surprisingly, physical fitness is, and always has been, highly rated not only at Sandhurst—where I had my nose broken for the third time in the boxing ring—but of course throughout the Army; and some of the keener wives take an active part, as evidenced by the following extract from 'Peterborough' in the *Daily Telegraph*:

A new standard of fitness, not for the Army's soldiers but for their wives, has been set by Susie Ross, the wife of the Commandant of the Guards Depot at Pirbright (and formerly the Adjutant at Sandhurst). She has been awarded a certificate for completing the Depot's assault course which is normally used for testing recruits to the Household Cavalry and Foot Guards. The wife of Colonel Malcolm Ross of the Scots Guards and mother of three young children went into training for the course with an hour's PT exercises every morning. She now plans to take up parachuting. An interest in fitness runs in the family: Mrs Ross's father is the man who introduced the tests when he was Director of Army Training in the '70s.

I think, on reflection, that my suggestion to Peterborough (for I was the source) that she was contemplating para or free-fall descents may not have been founded on fact, but

'Fit to Fight'.

the result was a flurry of media interest to the Isle of Wight where she was on holiday with her children (and the Colonel), in the hope of snapping her in training in her leotard!

The programme for these tests was called 'Fit to Fight'. I introduced a parallel scheme called 'Shoot to Kill', the object of which was to match physical efficiency with improved marksmanship.

'I don't care for that title,' remarked my wife. 'Too offensive and blood-thirsty.'

But what would she have preferred? 'Shoot to Miss?'

'Shoot to Kill'.

5

The Guards

From Coldstream, far north on the Tweed, one day
Two colonels came marching up London way,
Where, finding the Commonwealth losing tone,
They set Charles The Second upon the throne;
Then, asked about honours and due rewards,
They applied for the post of His Majesty's Guards.

This put His poor Majesty into a jam,
And he said 'I can't tell you how sorry I am
But I'm greatly afraid that this cannot be
As I've brought my Guards Regiment over with me,
And I think that the best I can possibly do
Is to call them the First Guards, and you Number
Two.'

This answer occasioned some justified ire,
And the Colonels replied—with forgivable fire—
'In our humble submission we cannot agree
As our motto is "Nulli Secundus", you see,
And if as the First Guards we cannot be reckoned
We'll be Third, Fourth, or Fifth Guards, but we'll never
    be Second.'

Lance Sergeant Henson, 2nd Battalion Scots Guards, training in Washington State, USA. This picture, taken by Staff Sergeant Thomson, Royal Army Ordnance Corps, was judged the Army Photograph of 1987.
Photo: Crown copyright HQ United Kingdom Land Forces, Salisbury, Wiltshire

So they left a wide gap where the Second should be,
Taking place—pari passu—as Number Three,
But to safeguard all claims they might otherwise lose,
They decided to wear all their buttons in twos,
And they said to the Scots Guards
'You stand where you please,
Provided you wear all your buttons in threes.'

When the Irish Guards came, after Africa's wars,
They naturally wore all their buttons in fours.
And last on the scene, the Welsh Guardsman arrives,
And he wears—Yes, you've guessed it—his buttons in
    Fives.
And all the time Coldstream said 'My dear old chap,
Don't mind about us; just step into the gap.'

Evoe, *Punch*, 1956

6

The Scots Guards

On 26 May 1990 a remarkable event took place in Edinburgh: a reunion of members of all ranks of the 3rd Tank Battalion Scots Guards, which had been reraised for service in World War II exactly fifty years before.

More than 150 were present, two of whom had come all the way from Canada. The Chaplain of the Battalion, the Very Reverend George Reid, a former Moderator of the General Assembly of the Church of Scotland and then aged 80, conducted a most moving service. During the address he said, 'Once a Scots Guardsman, always a Scots Guardsman.' So for me to claim that I served in that unique and distinguished regiment for 44 years is not strictly true; I am still serving and will do so till I die. Indeed, when I commanded the 2nd Battalion and we were presented with new colours at Holyroodhouse by the Queen, our Colonel-in-Chief, I said, in reply to Her Majesty: 'The fact that some on parade today no longer serve with the colours does not matter. What does matter is that we are all of us Scots Guardsmen, bound together in the Queen's service until we die by a chain the links of which are invisible, but which are as strong as steel; constantly striving in all we do to maintain the high traditions of loyalty and devotion to duty upon which the Scots Guards are founded; and sharing the motto of our Regiment which Your Majesty's grandfather once translated thus: "Beware of challenging the Scots Guards".'

The Queen's Birthday Parade. Her Majesty, escorted by her troops, returns down the Mall. *Photo: Sergeant Harding, HQ London District*

And it was this 2nd Battalion which was in the Falklands Task Force and fought so successfully and gallantly at Tumbledown Mountain, when they would normally have been taking part in the ceremony of Trooping the Colour on the Queen's Birthday Parade.

This regiment is a part of the Household Division and particularly of the Guards Division, comprising the Foot

Guards. Thus, in a sense, to write of one regiment is to write of all five, except that they each represent the national characteristics that make their soldiers 'different'—English, Scots, Irish and Welsh. All—potential officers, troopers and Guardsmen—pass through the Guards Depot, an experience never to be forgotten, where drill is prominent in the course curriculum.

COMMUNICATION DRILL

On commissioning, even young officers destined to serve in tanks were sent on a four-week drill course for potential non-commissioned officers at Pirbright. One of the features was 'communication drill', designed, we were told, to develop self-confidence, lung power and clarity. Officers were paired off for this improbable exercise, which it was hard to believe would be likely to contribute to Hitler's defeat. They were positioned at either end of a large barrack square, at least 200 yards apart, and under the eye of a drill sergeant ordered each other to execute quite tricky drill movements. The whole remarkable event was further complicated by the fact that at least half a dozen other pairs were simultaneously attempting at the tops of their voices to do the same. 'A very poor effort, Mr Gow, sir. You're just whispering', once greeted my efforts.

A BATTALION DRILL PARADE

When the 3rd Tank Battalion Scots Guards was stationed at Thoresby Hall during the War, the Commanding Officer held a drill parade for the entire Battalion every Saturday morning. A regular feature was that all officers junior to the Adjutant fell in under the Drill Sergeant, of whom there are two in each battalion. (In the Falklands operation one in the 2nd Battalion was killed in action.)

About twenty of us were put through our paces at an extremely rapid rate in what was called 'close order drill' until we were as exhausted as the rest of the Battalion, who were engaged in the same activities. When, at length, the Commanding Officer became bored with our efforts, everyone was formed up by squadrons and troops, preparatory to a spot of 'battalion drill'. I would doubt

64

whether these manoeuvres are carried out today, but young officers after the War were certainly expected to understand them, as sometimes they featured in the programme of formal inspections by senior officers. The following is an example:

Commanding Officer: 'Battalion at the halt, facing left, on
    number 1 troop, form close column of squadrons!'
Adjutant (*prompted by the Sergeant Major*): 'Mr Gow! What do
    you think you are doing?'
Me: 'Squadron Sergeant Major! Help! What do I do?'
SSM: 'For God's sake HALT, sir.'

I should add that I was not always the luckless one, and there were many who subsequently in both war and peace achieved distinction but who incurred the displeasure of their seniors in failing to master what was doubtless of tactical importance at Waterloo but whose relevance in Tanks was illusive.

AN ABSENTEE SCOTS GUARDSMAN

One of the most singular incidents in the unrecorded history of the Scots Guards took place between the two world wars.

The King's Guard at Buckingham Palace was being furnished by a battalion of the Regiment, and at that time the sentries were posted outside the railings (it was only after World War II that they had to be withdrawn within the forecourt because of the crowds of tourists). It is related that when the reliefs were being posted, in *broad daylight*, and the NCO and his party arrived at one of the posts in front of the Palace, he found to his amazement that the sentry, who was about to be changed, had gone! A search was instigated and the man's rifle and accoutrements were found, neatly

65

positioned at the base of a tree in Green Park, but there was absolutely no sign of the 'body', who must have disappeared in tunic and bearskin. Investigations failed to find a single witness who had seen the man, and yet, incredible to relate, he was eventually tracked down in Scotland, whither he had travelled by train (presumably still in uniform), staying with his mother.

Her only comment, when told about her son's dereliction of duty, was 'Och, he was always a wee bit o' a *wilful* lad!'

The Foot Guards are sometimes referred to as the 'Hat Men', most frequently by the Rifle Regiments—known as the 'Black Mafia', partly because of their buttons. This may refer to a custom which was prevalent for many years of Guards officers wearing their hats at meals. Scottish regiments wear the Balmoral or Glengarry bonnet. Cartoon by Osbert Lancaster.
Reproduced by permission of the Estate of Sir Osbert Lancaster and John Murray (Publishers) Ltd

BLITZKRIEG!

One of the most outstanding officers in the Regiment, and indeed in the Army, was Major Sidney Cuthbert, our second-in-command. Had he not been killed in the Battalion's first action in Normandy he would undoubtedly have risen very high in his profession.

He was a brilliant trainer with a fertile mind. After Dunkirk he was serving in the Holding Battalion Scots Guards at the Tower of London. He had studied with diligence the successful German tactics, and when about to take part, as a fairly junior officer, in an exercise against an 'enemy' which included the Irish Guards, he decided to try to emulate the *blitzkrieg*. His orders were to surprise the foe by advancing under the Thames via the Blackwall Tunnel; he went to the Army and Navy Stores and bought enough roller skates to equip every man in his platoon, and at the critical tactical moment these were donned. With Sidney at the head they sped down the tunnel.

Unfortunately, however, the Irish Guards' intelligence was excellent. His opponent knew not only of Sidney's plan to use the tunnel but had by chance been in the same stores and overheard him ordering the skates! Accordingly the Mick in question went to another department and bought a quantity of piano wire. Alas, the Scots Guards' *Schwerpunkt* met with disaster, as the attackers fell over each other in a heap, caught by the wire!

MORALE

This, quite rightly, is an important subject. Visiting generals usually ask, 'How's the men's morale? Pretty good, eh?', and I have often wondered what the reaction would be if the reply were 'bloody awful!' (Reminiscent of my wife, who regularly asks the waiter, when she has perused the menu, 'Is the chicken dish [or whatever] good?' I wonder what else the answer might be!)

One way to ensure high morale was to arrange visits by concert and entertainment groups, some of whom were professionals (like Vera Lynn, later to be made a Dame) and other amateurs—and not particularly gifted at that. On one occasion the Battalion was entertained by the 'Bristol Players' who were enthusiastic but definitely in the latter category. The Padre, the Revd George Reid, in addition to his normal duties had been appointed Entertainments Officer, and sat in the front row, minus his clerical collar. In between the acts the comedian leapt on to the stage and introduced his next appalling joke with the words, 'And 'ere's another good one Captain Reid told me . . .', much to the increasing consternation of the poor, dearly loved chaplain, but of course to the delight of the rest of the audience!

A TALE OF AN RTO

I am not entirely sure that the officer concerned was in the Scots Guards, but it is probable, and he was certainly a Guardsman of World War I vintage. He had remained on the reserve and was recalled to his regiment in 1939. Because of his age, he was considered unfit for active duty and was appointed the Railway Transport Officer (or RTO) at one of the London termini serving the northern routes. He commandeered a railway carriage which was parked on a platform not used by the trains, and there he lived in considerable state and comfort. He had an excellent orderly who looked after his every need, and the platform beside his parked carriage resembled a miniature Kew Gardens. He enjoyed a first-class cellar, and his luncheons and dinners, despite the restrictions of war, became renowned.

Some of his brother officers, however, felt that it was wrong that he should be allowed to spend the entire war in this splendour, and that something must be done. Accordingly a letter was written on purloined War Office headed paper to the Railway Board, posting him as RTO Edinburgh, but adding that in view of his long and conscientious work he should be allowed to take his carriage with him. Of all this the RTO, of course, knew nothing.

One night while he was fast asleep, the night train was gently shunted into his platform; his carriage was hitched on, and when he awoke in anticipation of his customary cup of tea, to his astonishment he found himself passing through the Border country!

AN UNDERGROUND STATION

Officers of the Foot Guards were formerly taught—No! ordered!—that they should not travel by public transport (except the railway system) under any circumstances.

I was once invited to dinner in the officers' mess at Caterham, and, togged up in my scarlet mess kit, I set off in my car for a convivial evening. Unfortunately, the car broke down en route and I was unable to make it go another inch. There seemed to be no alternative but to return home to London where I lived. I noticed a nearby sign which said 'Tooting Bec Underground'. Seeing no other solution than to avail myself of this opportunity, I bought a ticket and stood on the platform awaiting the arrival of my train.

Fellow-passengers were amazed by my appearance, and one even asked me if I was wearing a newly designed official uniform of the London Passenger Transport Board. I would be interested to hear if any other officer has had this experience.

PARCELS

Carrying parcels was similarly frowned upon, and I remember a conversation I had with an officer who worked in the headquarters of another regiment. One day in the mess at Wellington Barracks, I said to him, 'Tell me, what would you do if you saw an officer of yours walking along a street in London wearing a cap and a hacking-jacket, carrying a dead pigeon?'

'Don't be ridiculous,' he replied, 'It's an absurd and quite impossible scenario!'

'Maybe that's what *you* think, but just suppose. What would you do?'

Very grudgingly he said, 'Well, if he was at duty in a battalion, I would report him to his adjutant.'

'But what if he was quite a senior officer? What then?'

'The whole question is absurd, but I would give his name to the Lieutenant Colonel who would, doubtless, take the action that he thought appropriate. But it's all silly and would never happen!'

'How wrong you are,' I replied. 'What I have just described, I saw last Saturday with my own eyes. It was in the King's Road, and the officer concerned was *your* Lieutenant Colonel!'

THE DESTRUCTION OF MYSTIQUE

There was a time when any form of publicity on the part of an officer of the Household Troops was frowned upon, but having been invited to appear on the TV 'Blue Peter' show, where I was billed as 'Uncle Mike', I had no such inhibitions and readily agreed to be interviewed by a national Sunday newspaper.

The meeting was conducted in the old officers' mess at Wellington Barracks by a charming lady reporter, who arrived with clearly preconceived ideas about what a Guards officer was like—confirmed by the fact that the first she encountered when she entered the barracks was wearing a bowler hat and a monocle.

'Tell me', she asked, 'where is your country seat?', and she was taken aback when I confessed that I did not own one; from that we moved on to the number of grand clubs that she assumed I frequented regularly, how often I played polo with 'royal personages', the size of my yacht at Cowes, and so on.

After a while I thought that the moment had come to put her straight, and so I spoke thus: 'Yesterday when I was parading in the forecourt of Buckingham Palace as Captain of the Old Guard during guard mounting, perhaps the crowds peering through the railings may have thought, like you, that when I got home to my house in Wilton Crescent, let us say, I would ring for the butler, Smithers, and say, 'Tell Pomfret to bring the Rolls round at 2.30 and take me down to Clapton Hall, my seat in the Shires—and warn the staff there that tonight there will be 16 for dinner.' Little did they know, however, that they could in fact have seen me peddling along the Embankment with a bundle of dirty linen tied on the carrier of my army bicycle, hot-foot for the Baby Ward nappy service!'

She was amazed, and the caption of her subsequent article read: 'The Guards Officer who's different'. It was the last issue as the paper then went out of business, but I received a letter from a retired colonel who wrote that I had 'destroyed the mystique of the Officer Corps'!

THE HYPNOTIST

One day when I was stationed at the Guards Depot, almost the entire staff and all the recruits were assembled in the gymnasium to watch a performance by a hypnotist. He was sensational, and among his many sensations was an attempt to hypnotise the entire audience. We were all told to lock our fingers together and hold our hands above our heads. 'When I count to three,' he said, 'you won't be able to unlock your hands'—and in the case of over thirty spectators he was right! One by one they had to go up on to the stage to be 'released'. It was a great *tour de force*.

The hypnotist was invited at the end of the show to the officers' mess for a meal, during which a waiter came in with an urgent call: would he please go over to the sergeants' mess at once as there was a crisis. What had happened was that the barman there, because of his duties, had been unable to attend the performance, and a member of the mess had described to him the mass hypnotism of the audience. 'We were told to lock our fingers and hold our hands over our heads like this,' he had related, 'and then this chap counted to three; he said we wouldn't be able to unlock them'—and not only did he demonstrate to the barman what he had described, but to his horror he found himself locked!

Our guest returned soon after, having effected his release.

STRIKE ACTION

When the 2nd Battalion Scots Guards were stationed at Chelsea Barracks in the late 1940s, before they were despatched to Malaya for the Emergency, in addition to carrying out the ceremonial 'public duties' they were involved in aiding the civil ministries whenever there was industrial action and their services were called for. On one such occasion, a strike at Smithfield meat market, the Guardsmen entered fully into the spirit of the operation. On the side of a military truck, loaded with carcasses, some wag had chalked 'Lieutenant Colonel the Viscount Dalrymple and Co., Meat Purveyors'.

Such a thing, I would safely bet, had never before been recorded in the annals of the distinguished Scottish family of the Earls of Stair.

EMERGENCY ACTION

In 1940, after the German invasion of Norway had forced their king to go to England, King Haakon was walking with King George VI in the gardens of Buckingham Palace. King Haakon asked King George what would happen if a team of German parachutists suddenly landed there.

His Majesty replied that the security plan was excellent, and to demonstrate rang the emergency bell. Absolutely nothing happened! The Captain of the King's Guard, who, it is said, was a Scots Guardsman, telephoned the police sergeant on duty at the Palace, who replied that he had not been informed that there was any enemy present. But eventually a detachment appeared at the double who then, much to the amusement of the two kings, thrashed the shrubbery more in the manner of beaters at a shoot than of men engaged in the pursuit of a dangerous enemy.

DUTY AT CHEQUERS

In the later stages of World War II a composite battalion was formed called the Westminster Garrison Battalion. It was stationed at Wellington Barracks and comprised companies of each regiment, charged with the tasks of carrying out public duties, providing guards at key points and protecting the Prime Minister at Chequers. It continued for a while after the War, when I joined the Scots Guards Company, commanded by my old friend, the late 'Chips' Maclean.

While during the earlier stages of the War the Chequers Guard was very important, when peace came the small camp in the grounds was occupied by companies in turn, as a change from the routine of the London ceremonial commitments. I cannot say that the three weeks that we spent there were arduous. Route marches occupied part of our time which, together with sports, saw to the physical welfare of the troops; while their minds were kept sharpened by visiting lecturers, one of whom was a Mrs Marsden-Smedley who, if she achieved nothing else, at least kept the guardsmen awake.

The Prime Minister and Mrs Attlee came down at the weekends, and when they brought any of their family, the young officers were detailed to play tennis with them and found that the PM had quite a devastating underarm serve. The Attlees were very hospitable and we were often invited to dinner, where the food was good but frugal.

The high spot of our stay was when all the company was asked up to the house for a film show. We assembled and were shortly joined by the PM; we sat waiting and waiting, and at length, predictably and in keeping with the tradition of the Regiment, the Guardsmen began to sing, to the tune of 'Oh come all ye faithful', 'Oh *why* are we waiting?'

The reason soon became clear: the noises from the projectionist's box quite obviously indicated, especially when he joined in the singing, that the operator was absolutely plastered!

Mr Attlee was *not* amused!

7
Regimental Headquarters
Scots Guards

Each regiment of the Household Division—The Life Guards and The Blues and Royals, collectively called 'the Household Cavalry', and the five regiments of Foot Guards—has a headquarters in London. The former is in the Horse Guards building, Whitehall, and the latter in Wellington Barracks, Birdcage Walk. Twice in my career I served in that of the Scots Guards, and I thoroughly enjoyed both tours in those beautiful and civilised surroundings, serving an organisation to which I have been and still am devoted. The following recollections relate to these tours.

AN IMAGINATIVE PROJECT

I thought it would be a good idea, and certainly first-class publicity and therefore a spur to recruiting, if a visit to Moscow by the Band of the Regiment and the Pipes and Drums could be arranged. A highly successful (and lucrative) tour had previously been made to the United States, but in *this* venture I could find no interest.

Major Peter Balfour, the Regimental Adjutant (and later Chairman of a major Scottish company and Vice Chairman of a national Scottish bank, and prominent in many other fields), hard at work in the Headquarters of the Scots Guards where he found the experience vital for the future. He is here being advised by the Superintending Clerk and (*off camera*) the author. Photo: Balfour Collection

I then happened to read in a newspaper that the Prime Minister (Macmillan) was about to go to the Soviet Union, and that on the agenda for his discussions with Khrushchev were 'cultural exchanges'. Without, as far as I can recall, any reference to anyone in higher authority, I wrote direct to the PM suggesting that when this item was reached he should propose a visit by the Scots Guards. I later saw the War Office file, the very first letter of which was mine, and I always regretted that, like some John Le Carré character, I had not photographed the contents. Minutes flew back and forth between No. 10 and the War and Foreign Offices, culminating in one personally from the PM to the Secretary of State for War, whose reply was memorable, deserving a place on the wall of my personal 'rest room'. It ended: 'Let us hope that this is the last we hear of Major Gow and his crackpot ideas'!

MORNING REFRESHMENT

Like most regiments and corps in the British Army, the Scots Guards have an officers' dining club; ours is called 'the Third Guards Club', for that is what we were called from 1712 until 1831. The Club Committee meets once a year in the headquarters, under the President—who, at the time of which I write, was a veteran of the Boer War: Colonel the Earl of Stair KT. I was *ex-officio secretary* and wanted the meetings to proceed smoothly and amicably, so I told the Superintending Clerk that we would have a rehearsal.

'Now', I said, 'when I ring the bell, that is the signal for you to enter with the sherry. Let's try that out.' I rang the bell and in he came with the decanter and glasses on a *tin* tray which was illustrated by a lurid picture of cattle grazing on Ben Macdhui, or some similar venue. 'For heaven's sake,' I exclaimed, 'that won't do. Lord Stair will have a fit. Make sure there's a cloth on it when you do it for real.'

The Committee gathered, business was in progress and at the appropriate moment I rang the bell. In came the Superintending Clerk with decanter and glasses, but to my horror upon the tray was a cloth on which, in large red capital letters, was the word LAVATORY.

PRIVATE TUITION

I passed the examination for entry to the Army Staff College partly by luck and partly as a result of a course run by retired generals employed by an educational establishment—and all by correspondence. Submission of my written work was unrewarding. On one paper was the comment: 'The only good thing I can say about your paper is that it was legible', while on another, corrected by a different tutor: 'I can't read a word! Quite hopeless!' The notes and précis supplied were a godsend, however, and either the old generals must have been psychic or maybe they set the real exam questions themselves. At any rate, they achieved a most creditable pass rate for their alumni.

Thinking I might make a bit of useful money for myself on the side by the same means, I wrote to brother officers in the Household Division who, I discovered, were about to sit the exam, offering a crash course in which each would receive personal advice and tuition, conducted in the Guards Club—from me! My fees were modest and my course comprehensive, and both I and my pupils were confident of success.

How wrong we were: to a man, they failed!

A TV APPEARANCE

The Lieutenant Colonel commanding the Regiment, who paradoxically held the rank of a full colonel, abhorred publicity. It was, therefore, surprising that he agreed to take part in a television quiz programme—and a live one at that.

The panel was shown film clips of events which they were then asked to identify. In his case it was of an auction at which a Scots Guards Victoria Cross was up for sale. The panel failed, and the Lieutenant Colonel had to explain the event at which the medal was bought at vast cost by the Regiment, as well as the history of the award and the circumstances in which it had been won.

As always, he looked immaculate in 'plain clothes'. Two days later I complimented him on his performance and asked if he had received any fan mail. Yes, he had; one letter from someone enquiring where he got his stiff collars from!

MODERN TECHNOLOGY

My predecessor as Regimental Adjutant was extremely keen. On handing over, not only did he brief me extensively on every aspect of the job—and listening to him it all sounded so complicated that I feared it would be beyond me—but he also left several tape-recordings on which were further instructions and advice.

'Now,' he said, 'there is one last thing which is very important indeed', and he turned to a shallow cupboard on the wall behind his desk: 'This is so confidential that it must *always* be kept locked.' And with great pride he displayed the contents: down one side of a board were the names of every officer in the Regiment, and along the top a calendar, by months, for the next ten years. Against each name and running across the board were coloured markers denoting what job each would be doing in the years ahead, and for how long.

'This is absolutely unique. No one else has got anything like it. It took about six months to work it all out and it's complicated—though, after study, self-evident. I won't go through it now, but examine it with care later.' And with that, he left.

During the following days I listened to his tapes, studied the files and thought that, with luck, I might just get the hang of it all. There was, I recalled, something of import that I had yet to look at—ah yes: the career planning board! I found the key and put it in the lock; but it jammed, and however gently I eased it to and fro nothing happened, so I gave it a sharp tug. Off the wall fell the whole thing, crashing to the ground, bursting open and scattering the contents all over the carpet.

So if there is any officer who thought (or still thinks) that his career has been a disappointment to him, perhaps he will now know why! (I should add that, without applying any modern techniques and by using simple arithmetic instead, I worked out that if everyone senior to me got command of a battalion for two years, I would be 72 before it came to me!)

HIGHER HEADQUARTERS

There are some sceptical officers who have been heard to say that the *real* foe is not the enemy but higher headquarters. The wise thing to do, as a company commander, is to get as far away from battalion headquarters as possible—and likewise, up the chain of command. Naturally those in higher headquarters do not take the same view as their subordinates, and like to think that they are essential and highly efficient. That is what I thought about headquarters Scots Guards when I worked there—though it should be mentioned that the five Foot Guards lieutenant colonels were collectively known as the 'Crazy Gang'.

It is said that one pre-war regimental adjutant was unaware that a certain battalion had left the country until he received a postcard from Shanghai. What *is* true, because I was present myself, is the following story about a Lieutenant Colonel on a visit to a battalion at Victoria Barracks, Windsor. His last port of call before lunch was the sergeants' mess, on leaving which he turned to the assembled company and said, 'Well, goodbye; see you next at Wellington.'

They were amazed; their destination was Germany!

HEADQUARTERS
SCOTS GUARDS
Wellington Barracks Birdcage Walk London SW1E 6HQ

PERSONAL SECURITY

It will not have escaped anyone's notice that we live in an age where no one is safe from the threat of a terrorist attack.

It has been the custom for Regimental Headquarters to write to members and to address envelopes to their home addresses using military rank and including decorations of retired officers if appropriate. This could potentially reduce personal security.

Therefore I have been told to ask retired officers if they would like their names civilianised on envelopes we send out from here. ie Major General Sir Marmaduke Belloque-Ferox Bt DSO would become simply Sir Marmaduke Belloque-Ferox Bt and Major Gussie Bloodcurdling-Yell MC wold be G N P Bloodcurdling-Yell Esq.

To this end I would be grateful if you would complete the proforma at the foot of this page and return it to me at your leisure. We will presume that a nil return means we should leave things as presently shown.

R E WHYTE
Major
for Brigadier
Regimental Lieutenant Colonel

A sad sign of the times.

OFFICER RECRUITING

One of the responsibilities of the Regimental Adjutant is officer recruiting, and in this connection I once visited Radley College where my future brother-in-law, Brough Scott, was a pupil. I had written to him in advance, exhorting him to drum up some enthusiasm for what I thought an important occasion and one which might bring substantial benefits. I had a packed hall (but this, I discovered, was nothing to do with Brough; the Warden (or Headmaster) had declared that attendance would be compulsory).

I did not get off to a very promising start: I showed a film of the Queen's Birthday Parade, which was on two reels. Whether deliberately or by mistake, the operator got them muddled up, and part 2 was shown first, thereby throwing my riveting commentary into some confusion. I followed with a few well-chosen words relevant to the purpose of my visit, which I thought could not fail to move the listeners, and concluded with what, on reflection, was a rash note: 'If there is anyone who would like to ask me any questions or who wants further information about individual regiments, do not hesitate to stay behind.'

Almost to a man, there was a trampling of feet and they rushed from the hall. Only Brough stayed behind—'out of loyalty', so he said!

8
Command of the 2nd Battalion Scots Guards

To be selected to command a battalion is a signal honour, and there are some officers who in the past have wished for nothing else thereafter. I doubt whether this is the case today, and indeed a commanding officer of Sandhurst once told me that he was asked by a cadet what was the pension of a lieutenant general! Commanding Officer is the last appointment in which, unless you have an outstanding memory, you actually *know* all the officers and soldiers under your command. Moreover when I filled the post, I felt a responsibility for the welfare and happiness not only of the soldiers but of their wives and families as well, though in this day and age that view may no longer be applicable.

EAST AFRICA

I assumed command after the mutinies in Kenya and Uganda. The Scots Guards were fully committed to dealing with the former, and provided a company to go with another battalion for the latter.

It was *this* force that was ordered to fly into Entebbe and to secure the airfield for the arrival of follow-up troops. Accordingly, I was told, they landed and rapidly deplaned. As they charged to seize the control tower, they swept through a group of Africans who appeared to be in their path. Subsequently it was discovered that these were in fact the Ugandan Cabinet who were there to welcome them! It is said that the report of the Commanding Officer concluded, 'In the event this show of force was not strictly necessary. It had, however, a salutary effect upon all who beheld it.'

FAREWELL TO KENYA

Before we left to return home to England after Kenya had achieved 'uhuru' (freedom), it was decided that the Battalion should hold a farewell Beating Retreat at our barracks in Kahawa, just outside Nairobi. This was followed by parties held in the messes of the officers and sergeants, both of which were comparatively close to each other and similar in architecture.

A group of British expatriate guests arrived a little late in the officers' mess, and one of them apologised to me. 'Don't worry,' I replied. 'Very nice to see you anyhow, and I hope you've all got drinks.'

'I must tell you, Colonel,' said this guest, 'that by mistake we went to the sergeants' mess and we are rather sorry that we realised our error.'

Mystified, I asked him why.

'Well,' he said, 'it's very good of you to offer us gin and tonics and whisky here, but over *there* we could have dry martinis, Buck's Fizz, you name it!'

It just shows how the Army has changed—and, incidentally, soldiers stationed in some barracks in Germany now often live in flats where they employ a 'daily' to make their beds and keep the place clean.

A CLUB CHARACTER

When I was with the Battalion in Nairobi, the Muthaiga Club was a first-class establishment, and when I visited it ten years later I thought it was even better—and I should add that I became quite a connoisseur of clubs in outposts of what had been the Empire. When I die, if heaven is anything like the Mombasa Club was in 1964, all will be well!

One day in the Muthaiga I had pointed out to me an old man whose name, all these years later, I cannot remember; but he was a very well known character, and I hope that someone who reads this book will be able to tell me his name and confirm (or otherwise) the truth of this tale:

Many years ago, so I was told, this man fell in love with a British girl who lived with her family in Cairo. When he sought leave from her father to marry her, permission was refused. He was told to do something to prove that he was a 'proper chap'. So he went to Capetown and decided to walk the whole way to Cairo; and that is what he did.

On his arrival, he called at his girlfriend's house and was ushered in to see her father, to whom he related what he had done. The latter agreed that he had achieved something worthwhile and of which he approved. He was, therefore, prepared to give his permission, and the man must now tell the girl himself.

She was called for. The man had not, of course, seen her

85

for many months. 'By God, I can't possibly marry her!' he thought when he saw her, and fled.

RHODESIA

Our departure from Embakasi Airport was an emotional event. It seemed that the entire membership of the Caledonian Society of Kenya had turned out to see us off. The pipes played and the tears trickled down the wizened cheeks of these Scots who had lived for years in that beautiful country. 'What will become of us then you have all gone?' we were asked—and they compared our departure to that of the Roman legions from Ancient Britain.

'Well, I just hope I'll never be ordered to invade Rhodesia,' I remarked to the General, who was there to say farewell.

'What an extraordinary remark to make,' he replied. 'Of course that won't happen. Why did you say that?'

'I don't know,' I said. 'I just suddenly had a funny feeling.'

'Well, I wouldn't give it another thought if I were you.'

And yet . . .

U.D.I.

We had not been long back when in the aftermath of Ian Smith's Unilateral Declaration of Independence I was summoned late one afternoon to go up *as quickly as possible* to the Ministry of Defence. I arrived in uniform, which seemed to cause as much of a stir as if I had been dressed ready for a spot of PT. I cannot now recall who briefed me, but it was like a Staff College play and went something like this:

'Mark you, I told 'em all along that fella Rhodes wasn't to be trusted!'
Cartoon by Osbert Lancaster. *Reproduced by permission of the Estate of Sir Osbert Lancaster and John Murray (Publishers) Ltd*

Staff Officer 1: 'Right, Colonel, we've not much time as the Vice Chief wants to see you himself. Ready to take some notes?

Me: 'Could I have some paper and a pencil please'. (*This request, which the reader might assume to be pretty simple to satisfy in Whitehall, was, in fact, problematical, and both had to be sent for, thus causing delay.*)

SO1: 'Your orders are to stand your battalion to with immediate effect, the leading company at 24 hours' notice to move. You will emplane at Lyneham and you will land at Ndola. Clear?'

SO2: (*in confidential tones to his colleague*): 'I don't think that's quite right. Surely it's Lusaka?'

SO1: 'Look, I'm giving this briefing and I tell you it's definitely Ndola.'

SO2: 'I really think you ought to check.'

SO1 (*grudgingly*): 'Oh all right. Sorry about this, Colonel.' (*speaks to someone in RAF movements on the telephone*) 'Well, there seems a bit of a muddle. Movements say you may not know for sure till you've actually landed.'

Me: 'Well, let's just say it's Lusaka. What do I do then?'

SO1: 'Good point. I think you'll probably be ordered to move slowly to the Kariba Dam.'

Me: 'That's quite a long way, isn't it? I'll get transport, I assume?'

SO1: 'We haven't tied that up yet.'

Me: 'So that's why I'll be moving slowly—possibly on foot?'

SO2: 'If I were you, Colonel, I'd stay put in Lusaka or wherever and await developments. Ah, here's the Vice Chief's MA to collect you. Good luck, and rely on us!'

And that is roughly what happened! We remained on tenterhooks from the end of November till March, all packed up, but the remarkable thing was that all that time we still had to carry out the public ceremonial duties in London. (When I later told this to a member of the Army Board, he could not believe it.) I took one very practical measure. With some difficulty I obtained a street map of Lusaka, over which I pored with a magnifying glass. 'Eureka!' I exclaimed to the Adjutant. 'Guess what? There's a street in Lusaka called "Birdcage Walk"! What an omen! That's where we'll put the battalion headquarters.' Subsequently I discovered that it was the red light district!

Fortunately, in the event, as is well known, neither we nor any other unit was every sent to carry out this unspecified but doubtless most distasteful mission.

An interesting sequel was that I later met the Minister of Defence at that time, when he came to lecture at what is now the Royal College of Defence Studies. 'Yes, I remember you,' he remarked. 'I think we made a mistake then. We should have ordered you to go.' I asked him what I would have been expected to do. 'You would have flown straight in to Salisbury, disembarked, formed up with your colours behind the Pipes and Drums, and marched through the city. The sight of a well-disciplined, smart Guards regiment would have been greeted with cheers!'

'But just supposing that *you* were the Drum Major, marching at the head of the column, and instead of cheering crowds you found your way barred. What then?'

And the surprising solution was: 'Well, that would be *your* problem'!

AN APPLICATION TO GET MARRIED

When I wanted to get engaged to be married, the notice could not be published in the papers until I had formally applied for permission to my Commanding Officer, and provided that he supported the application, the ultimate sanction lay with the Lieutenant Colonel. I have a feeling that if my fiancée had been an actress, permission might well have been refused and I would have had to resign my commission if I had pursued the matter. (In fact my future wife had never trodden the boards, not even in a kindergarten panto, so all was well.)

My future wife may never have been 'on the boards', but I was (*centre*) with Michael McCrum (*right*), later Headmaster of Eton and subsequently Vice Chancellor of Cambridge University and Master of Corpus Christi. (As if that was not enough, he also published *Select Documents of the Principates of the Flavian Emperors AD 68-96*). This, however, was the Horris Hill play of 1936. On the left is Roger Weatherby, Commoner of Winchester College, where he was in the cricket and soccer first XIs; killed in action with the 6th Airborne Division east of the Rhine, 24 March, 1945.

Certainly when I was a Commanding Officer, Guardsmen were marched before me in order to obtain the same permission, and I remember one occasion well. I can't think what came over me; it is possible that the Regimental Sergeant Major had confided that in *his* opinion this particular man was too young. At any rate I said to him, 'Do you know that you are young enough to be my son, and so

I'm going to talk to you like a father.'

Looking back on it, I compliment myself on my kindness and eloquence: I spoke of the dramatic changes that would occur in his life ('Gone will be the days when you'd have been able to go out with the lads. . . The honeymoon doesn't last for ever . . .') Those who heared me were deeply moved when I came to the climax: 'Before you know where you are, there will be the added responsibilities of parenthood thrust upon you.' And I concluded: 'Think with care before you take this step', to which the Guardsman replied, 'I have, sir, while you've been talking. Thank you for speaking as you have. I now wish to withdraw my application—and he did!

What worried me, on reflection, as I told the Sergeant Major, was that the man's fiancée might sue *me* for breach of promise!

CEREMONIAL HORSEMANSHIP

The troops lining the Mall and the approach road to Horse Guards Parade on the occasion of the Queen's Birthday Parade are commanded by a Foot Guards Commanding Officer, accompanied by his Adjutant, both mounted. Their task is to ensure the proper deployment and alertness of the soldiers along the route, and once these are in position the two officers wait outside Buckingham Palace for the Queen's procession to depart. After that, all they have to do is to ride with dignity up the Mall to just short of Admiralty Arch, and then join the back of the column when the ceremony is over.

It might be deduced from this brief résumé that there would be little scope for mishap. But how wrong one can be.

When I was charged with this duty, my accompanying Adjutant was a nervous rider, but I was able to buoy him up with a deceptive display of self-confidence. At what used to be called the 'rehearsal' but is now called something different, to help him relax I said, 'I tell you what. As we've got plenty of time to get up to the end, let's just pop in to St James's en route and get a cooling glass of something from the mess sergeant of the Queen's Guard.' And this we did. We then went on our way, duly refreshed, with no mishap.

It helps if, like my wife, you were born in the saddle . . .

The day of the Parade itself started off badly. While I was waiting at the Palace, an important and obviously knowledgeable warrant officer of the Household Cavalry said to me, 'Lucky I spotted *that*, Colonel, sir. That curb chain is very badly fitted. Your charger won't like that one little bit after quite a short time. Make him *very* fidgety.'

'Well *do* something then,' I replied, but just at that moment out came the procession, and the opportunity had passed.

We satisfactorily circumnavigated the Victoria Memorial and were proceeding up the Mall according to plan, when my horse suddenly stopped. 'What do you think's wrong?' I stupidly asked my companion, who of course had no idea beyond suggesting, 'I think he remembers that last time we nipped into St James's at this point and he got a lump of sugar.' We certainly could not do that now as the crowds barred the way, but nothing I could do would persuade my steed to advance. (I had, I thought, been told on the equitation course that application of the spurs induced forward movement, but all that happened was that we went backwards.)

. . . or you can progress, like one of my daughters, to this. *Photo: Clive Hiles*

The restiveness of which I had been warned then became apparent, and this was transmitted to the Adjutant and his charger. At this moment the spectators became involved, and there were shouts of 'Ride 'em, cowboys', accompanied by other gratuitous remarks.

All this seemed to go on for a long time—so long, in fact,

that I thought we might still be there when the great procession marched back down the Mall. Luckily I spotted a mounted policeman whom I was able to summon. 'Help us, please. I can't think what's wrong with this horse. He won't move forward. Why's that?'

'Oh he wants to pass sir,' I was told.

'Well why doesn't he?'

'Only does it on grass, I expect. Some horses are funny like that.'

'There's none of that in the middle of the Mall', I replied, so we were led across the pavement as the crowd made way; the calls of nature were met, and to the cheers of the spectators off we set again and successfully reached our destination on time!

CHRISTMAS AND THE SERGEANTS' MESS

Both Christmas *and* Hogmanay are marked by festivities in the Scots Guards, and a major feature has always been a function to which officers are invited to the sergeants' mess and at which the 'Christmas draw' takes place.

'Do you know,' I remarked to the Regimental Sergeant Major, 'I've been attending these draws for more years than I can remember and I've never drawn a prize.'

'Well, sir,' he replied, 'there's always a first time.'

Come the evening and the draw took place. Suddenly the NCO in charge called out: 'Number 33 . . . The Commanding Officer! Well done, sir.'

'There you are,' said the Sergeant Major, 'miracles do happen'. to which I replied, 'Yes, Sergeant Major, but this really *is* a miracle. I never bought a ticket!'

9
Commander 4th Guards Brigade

Her Majesty's *Regulations for the Household Division*, the first edition of which was published over the signature of Prince Albert, Senior Colonel, in 1853, specifically says that when two or more Guards battalions are together in the same formation, that formation should be designated a 'Guards Brigade'. Sadly, when for a short time the Army was reorganised and brigades were abolished, not only was the 4th Guards Brigade the first to go but when the former designation was reinstated it was the only brigade that was not given back its title. This is a matter of deep regret to many members of the Household Division.

I am very proud indeed to have been appointed to command the only Guards brigade in the Army at that time. We were stationed in Germany, and the following anecdotes refer to my time in command.

A MATTER OF MODESTY

My wife was insistent that when I became a brigadier I should not be pompous. I think someone may have told her of the fairly lengthy correspondence that I had had with a friend in the Ministry of Defence whose department dealt with matters of rank, ceremonial and precedence. I had claimed that because, in World War I, officers who commanded brigades were 'brigadier generals', then I was now a general. In the event, however, it was decreed that I was not.[1]

Before I and my headquarters sallied forth for manoeuvres I discovered that I was expected to share the latrines with other officers, and I told my staff (and my wife, who thought I was being silly) that at my age I simply must have a private one. This was duly manufactured, but when we took to the field I saw that it looked just like one of the sentry boxes outside Buckingham Palace. I ordered that it should be redesigned so as to blend with the natural surroundings (woods, where it was fashionable at that time to site headquarters).

For the next manoeuvres I was shown with pride a latrine just for me which was beautifully designed to look like a tree. It was a work of art, and I asked for a photographic air sortie to be flown over the area so that the efficiency of our camouflage could be judged. When later I examined the

---

[1] In the passage outside the office of the Chief of Staff, HQ British Army of the Rhine, are two doors: one is marked 'Officers' and the other 'General Officers'. When at last I was promoted to the rank of major general, there was no doubt that I had reached the status that I had previously claimed. One of the first things I did on appointment was to fly by helicopter on a liaison or courtesy visit to the C–in–C, but in fact the whole purpose was to use the second of the above-mentioned doors. I imagined that the little room would be sumptuously appointed; there might even be a copy of the *Guards Magazine*! But *what* a disappointment; both soap and towel had been forgotten, and I had to move back to my old abode next door!

photographs, I saw that the concealment was excellent—marred only by a clear view of a somewhat large figure emerging from inside a tree!

JERSEY PULLOVERS

Orders were issued by 'higher authority' that name tags were to be stitched on to the jersey pullovers worn by soldiers of all ranks. (Needless to say, dashing cavalry regiments declined to wear the standard khaki issue, preferring specially made ones of traditional regimental colours, whatever that might mean. Even the chaplains followed suit and wore black.)

It was a simple matter for me to have GOW displayed on my bosom, but for others it was more difficult. One of my staff was named Blundell-Hollingshead-Blundell!

A staff officer calls to say goodbye to the Commander.

97

A TRIP TO BERLIN

I decided to take my family to Berlin for a few days leave, but when we got to Helmstedt on the border between what then were West and East Germany my car broke down. I left it to be repaired and we travelled up in comfort in the famous military train, a traditional feature of which was that a boiled egg was always served with the tea.

We had an enjoyable time visiting my old haunts, and thought that we would return on the same train and collect the car on arrival at Helmstedt; unfortunately, though, some keen REME corporal had not only decided to get it mended, but actually drove it up to Berlin and delivered it back to us. I was therefore faced with having to drive the family back down 'the Corridor' through East Germany to Helmstedt, a journey I had not done since 1945 when things were very different.

On arrival at the check-point on the western outskirts of the city, I had to visit the military police post to be briefed—and this was done by a WRAC staff sergeant who looked old enough to be my mother. 'Right, sir,' she said, 'now as you've never done this before, pay close attention . . .' And off we went with lengthy and, I thought, very complex instructions. I could see that it had all the makings of a disaster, and after five minutes I said, 'Stop!' She looked at me in surprise. 'If you tell me one more thing, I'll forget what you told me at the start.'

'What rank did you say you were, dear?'

'Brigadier,' I told her, to which she commented, 'Well, never mind'!

By the time I returned to the car, the family were well and truly fed up. 'Whatever have you been doing?' asked my wife. 'We've been here for simply ages. For goodness sake get on.'

I sat behind the wheel and started the engine.

'Come on. What are we waiting for now?' asked one of the

family.

And to this I regret to say that I had to tell the truth: 'Sorry, I can't remember what I have to do first.'

How we got back I can't think!

EXERCISE PARSONS' PLEASURE

An annual event in the military calendar of the British Army of the Rhine was (and perhaps still is) an exercise for all padres. One year the organisation of the 'practical' parts of Parsons' Pleasure—for such was its name—fell to me, and included an orienteering test. I was helped by a very senior member of the Royal Army Chaplains Department, who decided that he should check each padre who passed us en route to ensure that his pack contained all the specified items, one of which was a flask of communion wine. He was a perfectionist and a stickler for detail, so he checked not only that the flask was there but that it was full. Indeed, he went even further and decided to test the strength—in case, I suppose, some cleric had decided to sustain himself and then top up with water.

I cannot recall how many padres were submitted to his test, but by the end my fellow-judge was in very cordial shape.

It was this same padre who visited the Pony Club camp, attended by the army children of fathers of all ranks. It was a Sunday, and he was asked to take a simple outdoor service for the kids, at which he decided to preach about the feeding of the five thousand. 'Now children,' he said, 'I expect you know the story well . . . What *I* think happened was that when Jesus was told that the people were hungry, He thought it a good idea if they were asked to contribute what they had got—like me now: empty all your pockets, and those who have Smarties will give to those that have none!

So come on! Get cracking, like in the Bible.' One or two of the smaller people were at once reduced to tears and had to be removed!

COURTS MARTIAL

A friend of mine was once detailed to be a member of a court martial at Pirbright, which was to be held on a day when he particularly wanted leave to go to a race meeting. His request to be excused was promptly turned down by the Adjutant, but then my friend had a brainwave. As he went into the courtroom, on passing the accused, who was standing there, he murmured, 'Just you wait! I'll make sure you get a stiff sentence.' It was, therefore, hardly surprising that when the accused was asked by the President of the court if he objected to any of the officer members, he stated an objection to my friend, who was promptly replaced by another—and off he went to Ascot.

I was once appointed President, and I subsequently invited to tea in the Officers' Guardroom at St James's Palace the clerk[1] at HQ London District who specialised in proceedings. With his help and advice I went through the papers, ensuring that when they were submitted to 'higher

---

[1] Clerks in military headquarters can be very important and useful people. A friend once shared an office with me in Headquarters London District, where we were staff captains dealing with administrative matters. There was a third officer in the room who was from the same regiment as ourselves—keen and exceptionally earnest. My friend and I devised a plan: we used to get in twenty minutes or so before our colleague so as to go through all the files and papers for the day, choosing, on the advice of our friendly clerk, all the easiest ones. As a result, we finished our labours by early afternoon and departed, leaving the third officer hard at it. He can only have assumed that we were much cleverer and more competent than himself!

authority' they were in apple pie order. As a result, my performance was highly commended.

Years later, when commanding the Guards Brigade, I did a foolish thing. I happened to go into the mess and by chance met the Judge Advocate who was lunching there during a trial in my garrison. 'Do you know,' I told him, 'my name, apparently, has been put on a special list of officers qualified to preside at particularly tricky courts martial.' The legal luminary congratulated me, and I thought no more about it (except to wonder subconsciously why I had in fact told him this, which, on reflection, I was not even sure was true!).

Some time later retribution descended, and I was indeed 'specially selected' for what was a most complex case. On my arrival, the Judge Advocate and the civil barrister engaged by the defence both said how pleased they were that it was *I*, with my wealth of experience, who had been chosen for the task. Indeed, the former remarked that obviously there was no need at all for him to give the customary briefing on procedure, as I must know it all— and more.

All went well until nearly the end when I announced in a firm and confident voice, 'I now order the court to be closed for consideration of the verdict,' whereupon the Judge Advocate cried, 'No! No! I must sum up.' To this I stupidly replied, 'Oh. Is that strictly necessary?'

Fortunately no travesty of justice was, in the event, committed, but my services were never called for again.

10
Commander 4th Armoured Division

After a spell in the Intelligence Community, with which for many years thereafter I was associated as Colonel Commandant of the Intelligence Corps, I was retained in Germany, much to the chagrin of my wife, to command one of the three armoured divisions which were the British contribution in the Corps assigned to the Northern Army Group of NATO.

THE IRON HORSE

I was assisted in my responsibilities by a very efficient staff, one of whom—a full colonel—was in the logistical and administrative branch. I have happy memories of our association: On one occasion he accompanied me the whole way from Herford, Germany, to Fort Leavenworth in the USA, where for two days we did a sort of Morecambe and Wise show, explaining to a high-powered US Army audience how a British division was organised, commanded and administered.

At the close a lunch was held in our honour, and the Assistant Commander of the 4th US Division presented me with a 'small memento' which, he reckoned, would demonstrate the close association between our two similarly numbered formations. What he was about to give me was the symbol of his formation, which was called 'the Iron Horse Division'. I imagined that this fairly large model of a quadruped would be of *papier mâché*. But I was wrong: it was indeed of solid iron—and weighed a ton!

I was, however, able to say, 'Gentlemen, take my advice. A successful commander is he who ensures that he is served by a first-class staff to whom he can delegate with complete confidence. I therefore entrust this token to Colonel Millman who will *personally* ensure its safe passage back to our base in Germany,' and handed it to the gallant Colonel, who staggered beneath its weight.

MADE FOR THE PART

The same colonel was, I think, responsible for the production of a play, put on by the Headquarters for the benefit of the troops of the garrison and their families. I was a little hurt that my services had not been called for; I had fancied myself on the boards. However, there was no need for hurt feelings, it seemed. 'There's one part,' he confided 'which we thought might be just up your street, General. You'll see it right at the start of Act 2.'

I waited with keen anticipation as the curtain rose on an empty stage. Enter right: a butler. He moved left, picked up an ashtray; moved right, off stage . . . and never appeared again—and that was to be me!

SIXTH SENSE

Sixth Sense was (and may be still) a paper originally produced by the 6th Brigade Headquarters (hence the name), but at the time of which I write it had achieved greater status, having become the paper of the British Army of the Rhine.

As an historian, I am always grieved when I hear that original source material has been wantonly destroyed (like that of Queen Alexandra) or indeed massacred (like Queen Victoria's diaries, by Princess Beatrice). So it is deeply regrettable that there is no extant record of the contributions of two writers to this paper. For over a year Colonel Millman wrote under the pen name 'Max Comfort', always solicitous of the welfare of the troops, while I, the Divisional Commander, was 'Mabel Crump—the Woman behind the men behind the guns', thinking of 'our lads in khaki and two shades of blue'. One article by Mabel, I recall, was entitled 'Hints on how to treat your Hubby when he gets back from NI [Northern Ireland] for R & R [rest and recuperation]'.

What gems have been lost for posterity! But in retrospect I cannot help wondering what Lords Roberts and Kitchener would have thought of a major general doing such a thing!

A DIVISIONAL COOKERY COMPETITION

As something of an expert in the field of military cuisine, I took a personal interest in my Division's cookery competition, and made sure that my wife was equally enthusiastic. (When we married she had only two dishes in her repertoire—'cheese dreams' and bacon roll— but had progressed since then.)

We visited the gâteaux section, where she stood admiring the marvellous icing at which members of the Army Catering Corps excel. 'I've never seen anything so superb in all my life,' she remarked to one of the judges. 'I'd love to taste that one.'

'*Taste* it!' he exclaimed, 'That's the last thing you want to do.'

And the truth was out: though the icing changed, the basic cake appeared year after year!

My wife opened a new families' shop for servicemen. Official (*left*) thinks: 'That pineapple doesn't seem too good—*and* she's nicked some tomatoes by the look of it!'

THE TALE OF A TIE

As Colonel Commandant of the Intelligence Corps, I was very proud to be associated with the real military professionals, as evidenced by the very large number of honours and awards which have been, and still are, awarded to them, in their specialised fields. My position also allowed me to retain links, both national and international, with the Intelligence Community. I appreciated particularly my long association with the Government Communications Headquarters, or GCHQ, and I remember that on one of my many visits I remarked to the Director of the day that I thought he ought to introduce a special GCHQ tie, which would enhance the *esprit de corps* in his organisation.

Sometime later I was sitting in my divisional command post during an important exercise in Germany, when there was a knock on the door. In came the GCHQ liaison officer with a package addressed to me and marked TOP SECRET. YOUR EYES ONLY. I opened envelope after envelope until at last the contents were revealed—a tie!

Naturally on my next visit I wore it. 'Hello,' said the Director. 'Fancy you wearing that tie!'

'Well I must say,' I replied, 'I feel honoured to wear the tie that I suggested to you.'

'That's not ours. In fact we haven't thought one up. That is the tie of the Civil Service Sports Association, Western Region.'

Aghast, I asked, 'Do you mean to say that if I were wearing it in Cheltenham and saw someone similarly dressed coming the other way I could say to him, "First batsman in, Customs and Excise?", and he might reply, "No, outside right, Inland Revenue"?'

'Yes,' said the Director.

What a disappointment!

106

11
Life in the Ministry

The responsibilities of the Director of Army Training (or DAT), an appointment which I filled for three years and which I think has been abolished in the latest reorganisation of the Services—such reorganisations delight politicians of every hue (and a few soldiers too)—were wide-ranging. I cannot, however, claim that they were so heavy as to cause me to suffer a nervous collapse, which was suffered by an illustrious predecessor—Major General, later Field Marshal Earl Haig of Bemersyde.

The job had its moments, as illustrated by the following recollections.

A SUMMONS FROM A STANDING COMMITTEE

I knew next to nothing of the workings of Whitehall and the Ministry of Defence. It was explained to me that boards and committees were (and probably still are) all the rage, and the most important of the latter was, I was told, the Standing Committee on Army Organisation (SCAO). Staff officers spoke of it in bated breath, but I—fortunately, I thought—was not a member.

One day, however, I received a summons to one of its meetings, so I made a careful note of the number of the room where it was to be held. (In my experience it is not difficult to attend a meeting while failing to realise for quite some time—or indeed, at all—that it is not the one you should be at). The deployment of military manpower was to be discussed—a popular subject which afforded ministers an opportunity to show, once again, that by reducing the number of soldiers at duty, not only would money be made available for more false teeth, at cut price if not free, but the Army would emerge still 'leaner', 'fitter' and more 'cost-effective'. And there were some who actually believed this! As an important part of this exercise, I was instructed: 'DAT, you are to cut the training organisation by 10 per cent. Go away, work it all out and report back to us in a fortnight.'

Alas, it was all beyond me! If I so much as suggested that the Army School of Catering should sacrifice half a dozen instructors in the pastry department, there was a rumpus; when I suggested to the Director of the Royal Armoured Corps that a course called the 'Long Armoured-Infantry' should be abolished, I was told that by doing so I would be ringing the death knell of tank technology in the British Army for ever—'And who invented the tank in the first place: us!'

SCAO was glum when I reported back: 'They're not at all pleased with your efforts, you know,' remarked a senior civil servant before the meeting began. And the upshot was that I was told to try harder with a target reduced to 7 per cent. Again I failed, and I further failed at 4 per cent. It was implied that they might be left with no alternative but to report my sorry performance to the Army Board. Ministers, I was told, would be far from 'content' (one of the MOD buzz words), and there was even a possibility that No. 10 might be informed.

Life, however, is full of quirks: at the end of the day not only did I survive *en poste*, but my training organisation *increased* by 2 per cent!

'JOINTERY'

The Defence Training Committee had, as its principal members, myself and my opposite numbers in the Royal Navy and RAF. Our task was to see whether we could not do more things together—or 'jointly', in the popular jargon. A cry that was often voiced was 'A cook is a cook is a cook', and this from keen, ambitious officers who envisaged the setting-up of a tri-service school of catering—and why not indeed? But the obstacles seemed overwhelming at the time. Well, then, what about the chaplains? Alas, no headway was made.

A new admiral was appointed to the Committee, and as by then I had become the longest-serving member, he came to visit me. The following conversation ensued:

Admiral: 'I understand we sit together on the DTC?'
Me: 'That's right.'
Adm.: 'I've glanced through some of the papers' (*typical keen chap, I thought*) 'and I can't see one single thing that you've achieved.'
Me: 'You may be right. It's a very complex area, you know, but we try.'

It's no good just sitting behind a desk. Staff officers must get out 'on the ground' with the troops. The Director of Army Training (myself), lightly disguised as a 'Jock', about to go on patrol in Northern Ireland.

Adm.: 'Well I thing it's pretty pathetic and I'm going to sharpen things up a bit.'

Me: 'Oh good, you do just that. Splendid! By the way, I see we've got a meeting next week and I'm going to table a proposal that will be just up your street. It's pretty revolutionary, but I'm confident of your support.'

Adm.: 'I'll do my best. What is it, incidentally?'

Me: 'I'm going to propose that all basic naval recruit training should be done at the Guards Depot.'

Adm.: 'You can't be serious!' (his eyes bulged; his face became suffused with red) 'It's the most ridiculous idea I've ever heard. You must be mad. Their Lordships will be horrified.'

Me: 'There you are; what did I tell you? It's not as simple as you first supposed. But what's your objection?'

And he replied, in all seriousness, 'Well, we salute differently, for a start!'

THE EDUCATION OF OFFICERS

Considering the effort made at school to teach English—and the financial cost to those parents who chose to spend a great deal of money on private education—it was (and probably still is) sad that the standard of English writing of the British students at the Army Staff College was so poor. The Royal Military Academy Sandhurst tried to correct this shortcoming, but in my judgement it had been left too late. The fault, I deduced, must lie in the educational system. Accordingly when, as DAT, I addressed a conference of headmasters, I spoke about this with some vigour, giving examples and exhorting them to action.

A few days later, as I entered a lift in the MOD, I noticed a lieutenant general and a brace of major generals glaring at me in a distinctly uncordial fashion. 'Hello,' I said, 'Well here we are at the start of another fun-packed day!'

'Were you referring to me, by any chance?' asked the senior of the trio, brandishing his daily paper. I was mystified.

'Yes,' added another, 'I think saying that sort of thing in public is not at all the thing.'

I had no idea what they meant until I saw the article that was the subject of their displeasure. It began:

HEAD ARMY TRAINER SLATES TOP BRASS

General Gow, Director of Army Training, is highly critical of the illiteracy of his fellow-generals. Addressing a conference of headmasters, he said, 'I never cease to be surprised by the number of senior officers who do not appear to know that a sentence in English starts with a capital letter and ends with a full stop.'

FILM MAKING

I thought it would be valuable, historically and for training purposes, to record soldiers of distinction, while still *compos mentis*, who had some wisdom and experience to impart. The first of these films, or tapes as they later became, was entitled 'Templer in Malaya'. In it the Field Marshal was interviewed by a soldier and an academic about his time as Director of Operations in Malaya during the Emergency. This was followed by 'Monty and his Staff', featuring General Sir Charles Richardson who had served with *that* Field Marshal from the Western Desert to the Baltic. These films were shown initially to invited audiences from the MOD (thus bringing most of the Army Department to a halt), then widely throughout the Army.

It was after watching the second film that an extremely senior officer remarked, 'I think they are a waste of time.

Much too long, and anyhow everyone knows all about them.'

'I'm sorry, Field Marshal,' I replied. *'You* may know it all, but they aren't designed for you.'

He was not placated: 'Well anyhow, they're much too long,' and he stalked off in a huff.

Time passed and I happened to meet him in a London street. 'What's happening with your films?' he asked.

'Well actually, nothing. I can't think of a suitable star for the next one.'

'Really? What about me?—"The Armoured Regimental Commander" and "The Armoured Brigade Commander"?'

'Yes,' I mused, 'I suppose we could knock something up for, say, a total of fifteen minutes.'

'Fifteen minutes!' he exclaimed, 'That's ridiculous! They would have to be two completely separate films, each *at least* half an hour long!'

You can't win!

A VISIT FROM OVERSEAS

A military delegation from a Middle East country came to visit my department, but why they wished to see me no one seemed to know—not even the Foreign and Commonwealth Office. Their leader spoke no English; in fact, he did not speak at all, and the rest of the party was equally silent. Coffee was produced, and the situation became a little embarrassing, so I held forth slowly and deliberately for the benefit of the interpreter on every aspect of British Army training that I could think of. I was about to embark on the enthralling topic of higher staff training—and by this time I had got into my stride—when the leader suddenly held up his hand and spoke.

'The General tells me to say that we must go now,' said the

interpreter. 'We return to our Country in three days time and he will take back copies of every training manual on every subject produced in your Army.'

'Please tell your General,' I replied, 'that I'm not sure I can manage that at such short notice. I'm not sure, either, how many manuals that would add up to, but certainly several hundreds if not thousands. I'll just have to see what I can do and have them sent round to your Embassy.'

This was then translated and clearly ill received, but I shook them all warmly by the hand and ushered them out.

Within seconds, however, the door reopened and one of the visitors reappeared. 'My General is in great earnest about the manuals,' he said, in surprisingly good English. 'He has been ordered by the Minister of Defence, who is also the Prime Minister, to fulfil this mission.'

'As I told him,' I replied, 'I'll do my best. I'm sure he will understand if I can't get him the lot.'

'No he won't,' said the Staff Officer, wringing his hands in agitation. 'If he fails, he will be *shot*.'

Sadly, I can only assume that he was.

A VISIT OVERSEAS

I happened to meet a friend at a wedding reception in London, who told me that he was just off to Nigeria to set up their Army Staff College. 'What fun,' I said. 'If you're stuck for a lecturer, call on me.' And then I forgot all about it.

Some months later, however, he sent me an invitation to speak on 'Training in the British Army', and accordingly I flew out to Lagos, where I was met by the Defence Adviser, accompanied by a large person in flowing robes who undertook at once to deal with my baggage and formalities. I assumed that he was some sort of courier and was rather taken aback when he was ushered by an obsequious official into the VIP lounge and then joined us for coffee. Far from being a lowly courier, he was in fact a poet and the Commander of the Nigerian Brigade of Guards. Before I returned to London he presented me with a gramophone record of the music of the Guards March, complete with words which he had composed himself. He was well versed in the history of the British Guards Armoured division; one particular line went something like 'We march with one eye open and one eye shut'—referring to the 'ever-open eye' sign of that great formation. In a subsequent coup I believe this charming man was shot.

Far from lecturing only to the Staff College, I found that I was to address audiences of all the officers of the Nigerian Army! The first of these sessions took place just outside Lagos, and when later the Defence Adviser and I returned to his house, his wife remarked that a most unusual thing had happened: for once, the electricity supply had not been cut off. 'That's because General Gow was lecturing and using "visual aids" during his talk.'

'Steady on,' I riposted, 'that's ridiculous. You don't keep supplies going in the capital just because *I'm* giving a lecture?'

'You do here,' said the DA, 'if the President says he's going to come and listen in the audience—and he did!'

A ROYAL DISAGREEMENT

My efficient Deputy once said that he thought it might be a 'good idea' if we held a DAT conference to which would be invited all the members of the Army Board, the Commanders-in-Chief, and in fact all the 'top brass' of the Army, including that important personage the Academy Sergeant Major, Sandhurst. Such an event had never been

115

This cartoon was presented to me on my departure from the MOD as DAT. On the reverse, signed by thirty officers of my staff and dated 20 December, 1978, was the following:

> Some three years ago we were all rather slow
> When a Guardsman came out of the sun.
> His aims were quite clear and he left us in fear
> That training just had to be 'fun'.
> With ideas galore, he pushed open the door
> And got us all out on a run.
> From the reverse you can see, in fond memory,
> These projects he's begun and got done.

held before, nor, I think, has it since, and the Deputy was enthusiastic. 'Leave the detail to me,' he said, and of course I was delighted to do so.

When he had got well into the final phase of planning, and invitations had gone out, he remarked casually, 'On your behalf I've asked the Duke of Edinburgh to speak.'

Somewhat surprised, I said, 'Oh, do you think he'll want to come, and even if he does, will he really want to speak?'

'Yes,' he replied, 'I've just heard from his Private Secretary that he intends to address the conference on a subject dear to his heart: the creation of a special Military Studies degree course for non-specialist officers not doing a science or engineering course. Such a degree course, HRH maintains, would be of direct relevance to the military profession, unlike some subjects that are read.'

The conference opened, and I had done a certain amount of research on the subject of Prince Philip's choice, the outcome of which was that despite the merits of his proposal, neither the academics nor the officers themselves were enthusiastic (for reasons which, as far as this book is concerned, are neither here nor there). Thus it was that in the discussion period after HRH's address I felt it my duty to express these contrary views. I added, however, in order, as it were, to soften the blow, that I had not actually been to a university myself. This brought the inevitable and no doubt well deserved comment from our distinguished visitor: 'There sits the DAT, revelling in his ignorance!'

'My son, sir, was one of the very first university cadet entrants to be commissioned into the Army,' I added in order to recover the Royal Approval, 'and he became the Adjutant of a Scots Guards battalion.'

'And what did he read?'

Much to HRH's annoyance, I truthfully replied, 'Anglo-Saxon and Fine Arts!'

12
Scotland and Her Army

It is a unique fact that the general officer posted to what used to be called 'Scottish Command' not only has the rank of Lieutenant General but is also referred to as 'the General Officer Commanding the Army in Scotland'. When I had the honour and good fortune to be just that, I remember meeting at the studios of Radio Scotland a prominent member of the Scottish National Party, which had recently published a Defence White Paper.

'I don't suppose that you support us,' she said.

'On the contrary,' I replied. 'I've just read your Defence Paper and it is first class. I would be made a Field Marshal and Chief of Scottish Defence, so count me in!'

Here are a few recollections of my very happy time in post in my homeland.

THE BRIEFING

My predecessor was a very old and dear friend, from the same regiment as myself, and he invited me up to Edinburgh to be briefed on my new command and in particular to see how *he*, a super-enthusiast (and that is a mild description), handled the Military Tattoo. ('Do you know,' I was told, 'he attended every rehearsal and every performance!'; to which someone added, 'Yes, *and* he watched it on TV!')

My installation as Governor, Edinburgh Castle.

119

For the briefing he sat me in an armchair before what looked like an over-large television screen, while he mounted the podium from which he then addressed me alone. As he spoke, he kept flashing pictures on to this screen to illustrate his points. The session seemed endless, though of course invaluable.

Suddenly, rather to his annoyance, I stopped him in full flood. 'Can I just say three things? I *do* know a bit about the Army; I am a Scot and have lived here; and I simply must go to the loo!' Later I was told that he had altered his briefing. 'Oh good,' I said.

'Yes,' said my informant, 'he has tape-recorded his speech and now sits beside you, adding extra comments in person. Isn't that what's known as a voice-over tape?'

THE EDINBURGH TATTOO

My predecessor held very large dinner parties every night during the Tattoo for the distinguished person who was to take the salute, and he invited me along to see how he did it, as presumably this would be my lot in the future.

We had just assembled in the drawing-room when suddenly our host darted in—dressed as an Arab sheikh! 'Pay attention,' we were told. 'Now you are *really* going to enjoy tonight. All the participants are as enthusiastic as I expect you to be, so give them all the support you can. Now listen. When I've finished talking, you will all go in to dinner—and a jolly good one it is too. You will be told where to sit, and you have exactly 25 minutes to eat it. When I blow a whistle, that is the signal for you to go to the cloakroom—five minutes allotted for that—and then back in here again to be told about transport. I assume all that is quite clear, so have a good meal.' And off we were hustled.

Precisely 25 minutes later, there was a piercing blast on the whistle and out we all scampered. When we reassembled, there again was our host, but this time wearing a fireman's helmet!

I regret that by comparison *our* Tattoo dinners must have seemed very dull.

A VISIT BY THE CHIEF OF THE ITALIAN ARMY

One day I was told by my staff that the Ministry of Defence had rung up. The Chief of the Italian Army, with his wife and entourage, was paying a visit to this country, and we were required to look after them for a couple of days.

It was clear to me that a 'command decision' was required, so accordingly I telephoned the Regimental Secretary of the Argyll and Sutherland Highlanders (Princess Louise's Own) whose headquarters was (and still is, though in a different part) in Stirling Castle. 'Timber, rally round. Here is a moment that seldom comes your way!' And I explained the situation . . . 'Red carpet, give it the works; the honour of Scotland and your great regiment is at stake!'

Off we set in a fleet of limousines from my house, where the charming Italians had been staying, but by the time we arrived at the castle the rain was torrential. Unperturbed, 'Timber' Woods, the Regimental Secretary, had made his plan which *would* be adhered to: the party was handed over to the care of the chief guide (or warden) of the castle who, despite the inclemency of the elements, insisted on carrying out his programme. Huddled under umbrellas, our guests pluckily stuck it out, but they must have found the commentary incomprehensible, so strong was the guide's 'Doric'. His climactic words were: 'Caast yor eyes to the laift. What du yu think ye can see? A hole i' the wall? Thaat's nae hole. Thaat's wheer his late Maajesty King Jamie kept his Chateau Neuf dew pappy!' On that high note we entered the

121

RHQ and mess, passing through the museum on the way. It would have been hard to improve on the elegant ambiance.

While we were enjoying the aperitifs, suddenly there appeared the figure of the Colonel of the Regiment—the famous General Freddie Graham. 'Hello, what's going on?'

Sotto voce I replied, 'Head of the Italian Army.'

'Oh,' said the Colonel, 'I remember when we chased those fellows out of Sidi Barrani!'

'No! No!' I whispered, 'they're our allies!'

The food was magnificent, every course piped in, and our visitors duly impressed.

THE ORDER BOOK

Recalling this incident with the late Freddie reminds me of my first staff appointment after I graduated from the Staff College in 1955. I was appointed the Brigade Major (now called Chief of Staff) of a brigade stationed in Minden, Westphalia. At that time we were housed in a temporarily deceased coffee factory called 'Melita House', and I had been there for about a week when I noticed for the first time in my office a cupboard, on the top shelf of which, covered in dust, was the order book of a previous commander— Freddie Graham. I wish now that I had kept it because it was an historical document, quite apart from the fact that I had never seen a formation directed by the written word. Here is one example of what I mean:

Order 45.   DAA & QMG.   I will not tolerate one single man in the Brigade under my command whose bootlaces are done up criss-cross. FG

Order 78.   DAA & QMG.   Reference my Order 45, I have today seen two men whose bootlaces were done up criss-cross. Action. FG

He was indeed a remarkable man!

'Willy's just remembered that his maternal grandmother was a MacPheeble of that Ilk.' Cartoon by Osbert Lancaster. *Reproduced by permission of the Estate of Sir Osbert Lancaster and John Murray (Publishers) Ltd*

WHISPERS OF MORTALITY

There is a considerable amount of ceremonial from time to time in the capital city of Edinburgh, requiring the personal attendance of the three Service Chiefs: the Flag Officer Scotland and Northern Ireland, the General Officer commanding the Army in Scotland, and the Air Officer Scotland and Northern Ireland. One such occasion is when Her Majesty the Queen arrives at the Palace of Holyroodhouse at the start of the annual royal visit. The Lord Provost presents the keys of the city, and the Service Chiefs, together with the Chief Constable, stand in a line and are presented.

I had been a soldier for 38 years and was aged 56. Someone had once told me that at a certain age the first signs of mental frailty start to become apparent, but I reckoned that for me that moment had not yet come; I felt pretty sharp and alert. Just before the Queen's car was to sweep into the forecourt and the Guard of Honour was standing to attention in anticipation, a terrible thought came suddenly into my head—and it was in a sense quite ridiculous. I simply could not remember whether when *I* myself came to attention I brought my left foot into my right or vice versa! I racked my brains as the seconds ticked by, and at last found the answer. Instead of seeing myself in my present role as the Queen's General in Scotland, I cast my mind back to when I was one of the late King's Scots Guardsmen at the Depot, on the barrack square, and at once I had the correct solution!

It had given me quite a nasty shock, and I was glad that the Chief of the General Staff, whose visit was imminent, never knew of it, as it might have altered the outcome of the following anecdote.

SELECTION FOR FURTHER EMPLOYMENT

Luck largely dictates one's military progress. The Chief of the General Staff was staying, and after dinner he asked if we could go somewhere for a chat; so we repaired to my study.

'Now I've been thinking,' he said, 'what you might do next: either C-in-C BAOR or Adjutant General. What do you think?'

'Well,' I replied, 'honestly, we've spent such a long time in Germany that I . . .'

'Oh, good. I'm so pleased that you would like to go back.'

And that is how the decision was made. Had his hearing been better, I would have become the Adjutant General—but, of course, if he had known what had happened at Holyroodhouse I might well have become nothing at all!

13
The British Army of the Rhine and NATO's Northern Army Group

To command for nearly three years the only British Field Army outside the United Kingdom was a wonderful experience and a great honour. The NATO appointment went, as it were, with the job and had done so for many years, as had the parallel appointments of C-in-C RAF (Germany) and command of NATO's 2nd Allied Tactical Airforce. My RAF colleagues during my time there were personal friends—Sir Thomas Kennedy and Sir Patrick Hine—and together we welded our two organisations, national and international, more closely than had ever been achieved before. It was a very happy relationship and one that I shall always cherish, not least because we all shared a sense of humour!

A FLYING EXPERIENCE

I thought it important that I should learn at first hand what it was actually like to be an airman. I imagined, rather naïvely, that at any rate as far as air defence went, the pilot's life was still one of sitting around in a deck-chair, waiting to

At the end of an educational flight.

be 'scrambled' as in the days of the Battle of Britain. A visit to a Jaguar squadron of RAF (Germany) was, therefore, an eye-opener: this was a life for men much younger than I! I was taken for a flight the length and breadth of the Federal Republic, responsibility for the defence of whose airspace at that time still lay with the World War II allies.

When at last we landed back at base, my pilot said, 'Right, General, I expect you would now like to be debriefed?'; and he seemed surprised when I declined. 'Very unusual. A cup of coffee, then?', which I also declined. 'Well, what *would* you like to do?'

'Frankly', I replied, 'I feel so absolutely exhausted, I just want to go home!' Thank goodness, I thought, that I was a soldier; and my admiration for my airforce colleagues soared.

THE USE OF TELEVISION

With the installation of a TV network for British Forces Germany, my fellow-C-in-C and I were able to talk to every service man and woman, and their families, provided that they had a set and didn't switch off the moment they saw that it was one of us! We took it in turns to be the Chairman of the Commanders-in-Chief Committee, and whoever happened to be in post at the time spoke for the other, thus presenting an all-important united front.

During my tour the government decided to reduce what was called the 'local overseas allowance', paid to all service men and women in Germany, and because I happened to be 'in the chair' it fell to me to go on TV to explain the cuts and the reason for them. It was a complex subject which, try as I could, I found difficult to master completely. Furthermore, my heart was not really in it and I personally considered the reductions difficult to justify.

At the end of the rehearsal the producer suggested that I should try to round off the broadcast in an informal way, and asked me how I would do this. I thought it a silly question because if I worked it out in advance, it would lack spontaneity, so I just assured him that I would ad lib as the spirit happened to move me. At the critical moment, therefore, I concluded by saying, 'Well, there it is, and I can assure you that Air Marshal Kennedy and I really have tried our very best for you all, and it could have been worse. But I'll tell you one thing that worries me: my wife is in England and not watching this programme. I'm not at all looking forward to what she'll say when she gets back and hears! Goodnight, and wish me luck!'

The next week I went on a tour of my Command, and I thought I might have a rough time when I visited sergeants' messes and so on, but not a bit; all they wanted to know was what my wife had said when she heard the news!

THE C-in-C's WIFE

Some soldiers marry wives who revel in understanding everything military; they may even have served in the Army themselves. Others, on the other hand, know little or nothing, but still gallantly help their husbands to struggle through life.

Although my wife had served in the Royal Navy as a Leading Wren (visual signaller) and was a war veteran, by no stretch of the imagination could she be described as 'militarily minded'. She was a splendid hostess and did all the things that she was asked to, even though she had a tendency to drop off. On one occasion she did so in the middle of something rather interesting that she was saying herself, but no one minded; and she was, I think, a great support to my staff officers, both national and international, and their wives.

Ex officio she was the President of the International Ladies' Club at Rheindahlen, Germany, and as such once attended a demonstration of flower-arranging (at which she was herself very adept). She was met at the entrance on arrival— fortunately, on time—and escorted to her seat up front. After a while she murmured to the lady on her right, who was a friend and the wife of the Senior Air Staff Officer, RAF, 'When's the demonstration going to start?'

To which the reply was: 'It's about to finish!'

She had had a nice snooze throughout.

For a Commander-in-Chief, relations with the Germans are important. A visit down the pits in the Rhineland:
Myself (*left*): 'Are you the Arthur Scargill of Germany?'
Trades union leader (*centre*): 'Certainly not! I am the Joe Gormley!'

HIGH TECHNOLOGY

I once visited a regiment of the Royal Engineers in their barracks, which had been modernised so that every soldier either shared a room with a chum or had one to himself. One young sapper was very proud of his single accommodation, which was immaculate and dominated by the biggest and most complicated 'music centre' that I had ever seen. I assumed that he must therefore be very musical and was surprised when he said that he was in fact tone-deaf. Furthermore, he disclosed that the equipment had cost him a great deal of money.

'If you aren't musical, why did you buy it, then?' I asked.

'Well, sir, I've never in my life actually owned anything valuable, and at last this is it!'

'I'll tell you one thing,' I commented. 'Mark my words, if you ever get married, one of the first things that will happen is that you'll have to sell it.'

To which he replied: 'I know. I'm getting married next week!'

My house sergeant possessed two video machines while I had not one. There was a TV show that my wife particularly wanted to see while we watched something else, and the sergeant said he would bring one of his machines along so that we could record it. So round he came and showed me how to work it. I asked him if he was on the telephone at home (which he was) and whether he would be in that evening (and he said he would be). Was his car running all right? Yes it was.

'Why do you want to know all this?' he asked.

'Because I'm absolutely sure that I'll be quite unable to work this thing and may have to ask you to come back.'

'Never, sir,' he replied. 'After the explanation I've given you, you can't go wrong; it's dead easy. Why, your grandchildren could do it.'

'Maybe,' I said. 'They're of the high tech generation and

131

I'm not. Just see.'

And regrettably I was right, and had to ask him back at the critical moment!

The High Tech generation—four of my five grandsons.

And the granddaughters are pretty sharp, too—and said they weren't going to be left out of the book!

A VISIT BY A ROYAL PERSONAGE

During the years of the Cold War it would have been a safe assumption by Western Intelligence that the residence of the top Soviet general in what was then the German Democratic Republic was in a high security area. What the Warsaw Pact Intelligence and the Soviet GRU assumed about the British equivalent in the Federal Republic (me) I do not know. Had they known the full truth, I doubt whether they would have believed it!

Flagstaff House, remote from the large Rheindahlen Headquarters, was guarded night and day by members of the MSO, or 'Mixed Services Organisation'. They were mostly Yugoslavs who had supported King Peter and the non-Tito partisans, and who after the War could not return to their native land because they would be shot. There were members from other Eastern European countries as well, who for similar reasons could not go home and, as 'war veterans', were well past middle age. Indeed, as my wife would say, they were mostly in their 'twilight years'. Upon *them* depended the security of the C-in-C and anyone else who was in the residence, and as increasing age caused vacancies in their ranks it became difficult to recruit replacements. At any rate, there they were, inspected every morning by the C-in-C himself and providing a permanent sentry on the main gate, who was watched over by a 'Superintendent' and at night by an additional 'prowler' in the grounds.

A Royal Personage was about to visit the headquarters and would be staying at Flagstaff House. As a former Head of Military Intelligence and Security, I felt that I should pay personal attention to the safety of His Royal Highness while he was under my roof, so I selected as the Commander of the Guard the MSO Superintendent whom I reckoned to be the keenest and most reliable: a younger man, nicknamed by the family the 'Phantom Saluter'. This was because whenever he was on duty and spotted me strolling in the garden, he would track me, periodically popping out from behind the shrubbery to salute.

Unlike the Royal Personage, these veterans of the 3rd Tank Battalion Scots Guards had no difficulty when they popped in to Flagstaff House for a drink!

This man I briefed myself: 'Now this visit is very important. I expect a high standard of efficiency, smartness and in particular alertness at all times. His Royal Highness will arrive at the main gate tomorrow at 1830 hours precisely. His limousine will be *preceded* by a military police car, and you will turn out the whole Guard in his honour. Remember security! His Royal Highness is particularly hot on that. Do NOT let anyone else enter; they may be terrorists or saboteurs. Do you understand?' And I repeated it all in German, just to make sure it was *alles klar*.

'Sir General,' replied the 'Phantom', saluting several times, 'say no more. Alles klar! You will be obeyed!'

134

What more, I wondered to myself, need I do? And I concluded that it was all buttoned up.

I recall that I was relaxing in the drawing-room at about 6 pm. My wife was, as usual at that time of day, feeding the animals, and there was a general atmosphere of domestic calm. Suddenly this scene was shattered: the door opened, and in came . . . HRH! 'By God,' he cried, 'getting into this place is worse than Fort Knox!'

What had happened, I later discovered, was that the Royal Personage had got fed up with the carefully timed movement plan to my house and had told the driver to step on the gas, overtake the lead police car and press on. As a result the royal limousine arrived at my front gate (and the MSO Guard) well in advance of the stated time. This must have been the moment when the 'Phantom' saw instant promotion in the offing, and no doubt a medal for personal services and zeal. With hand on pistol he advanced from the guardroom, barring further forward movement. 'Who are you?' he demanded in broken English. 'You should not be here! I demand AT ONCE your passes'—and this to the passengers in the back who, hardly surprisingly, had none. 'So! You are dangerous assassins! You will go no further except to my guardroom!' . . .

How, in the event, the Royal Personage was extricated from this situation I cannot now recall, but I could not resist pointing out to His Royal Highness that we *did* try to keep on our toes, and that now that he had safely arrived he would without any doubt enjoy a secure and peaceful stay.

But alas, I had forgotten my wife's collection of bantams, which gathered beneath our visitor's bedroom window and launched off in a dawn chorus which resulted in an early reveille.

14
Recollections of 'Abroad'

Certainly British people of my grandfather's generation, and possibly even some of my father's, had a suspicion of 'abroad'. By this they did not mean visits to parts of the world which in Philips' Atlas were coloured red, because they reckoned that they were part of home—the Great British Commonwealth and Empire. They had in mind, *au fond*, Europe, which they admitted was interesting—with a few reservations—but from which they were always relieved to return. 'Ah, my boy,' said my grandfather once, 'there's nothing to beat the first glimpse of the white cliffs of Dover on return from "abroad".' Then there were all the problems of the different food. '*Never* drink the tap water when abroad,' cautioned my mother, and there were other very 'un-British' things to be encountered, such as 'duvets'.

It all seems an age ago since views like these were expressed—and expressed by quite intelligent people—and of course it *is*. Somehow the United States never seemed to be included in this category because, perhaps, the founding fathers came from these islands—and it was reckoned that there were more Scots in North America than in the ancestral homeland. So I choose to reminisce about the Americans first.

OUR AMERICAN COUSINS

I got to know a lot of Americans well and could claim them as close friends, and I hope (and believe) that they would agree. The British often fall into the trap of thinking that Americans are just like them, and then are surprised to find that in a number of respects they are *not*.

When once I was in Washington DC, visiting a bank in the Pentagon to cash a cheque, I asked the pretty girl behind the counter if she could give me an 'elastic' band to put round the notes. 'Excuse me, sir,' she asked, 'what was that you just said?', and I repeated it. 'Say, girls,' she exclaimed to her colleagues, 'gather round and just you listen to this gentleman! Isn't his ac-cent sure cute?'

MILITARY MISUNDERSTANDINGS

The Commanding General of a US armoured division in Germany came with a team to lecture his British opposite number and staff on the organisation and *modus operandi* of his formation. A map was displayed on a screen showing a tactical situation for an attack, and upon this was written the following: 'LD IS LC.'

Mystified, and never shy of displaying my ignorance, I said, 'Stop, please. What does LD mean?'

Answer: 'Line of Departure.'

'And LC?'

'Line of Contact.'

'Clear. And what about IS?'—to which the CG retorted, 'Boy, how dumb can you be? "I am, you are, he IS"!'

Somewhat abashed, I remained silent for a while until the General described how he actually commanded his troops on operations. 'Delegation' was not a word in his vocabulary, and he seemed to do *everything* himself. I remarked that he must sometimes get tired—I felt exhausted just listening to him! What happened when he had to have forty winks?

'No problem. I hand over to the ADC.'

This really mystified me. Thinking of my own aide-de-camp, I asked, 'Isn't he a bit young for the job?', only to be told that in US military parlance 'ADC' meant 'Assistant Division Commander'.

THE COMMANDER-IN-CHIEF
UNITED STATES ARMY EUROPE, OR CINCUSAREUR

The C-in-C (pronounce 'sink') was my opposite number when I was C-in-C BAOR. I had met a previous officer in that post, General Michael Davidson—when I was, in American parlance, 'Head of Intel'— who was kind enough to say about *his* and *our* military Intelligence organisations: 'We don't see here two, separate national intel set-ups, working independently, but one, truly *joint* staff'—high praise indeed. So I already had a rapport.

At that time he lived in a beautiful house in the hills overlooking Heidelberg, where I was invited to stay when I paid my first visit as a Commander. Our American friends work in a different time frame from ourselves, and before we went to bed, somewhat to my surprise, he said that breakfast would be at 0515 and that we would leave for his HQ in the limousine at 0530. And so we did. As we drove down the hill the first glimmer of dawn was scarcely perceptible, and I asked him if he had a back-up security car following. The answer was No. Was there one in front? No. Whereupon I told him that I would not be surprised if one day I heard he had been shot up by terrorists en route.

How prophetic I was, because *that* is precisely what happened, and he and his wife were nearly killed by a rocket attack. As a result, he later had to quit his grand mansion and move into barracks in conditions of considerably reduced splendour.

On this occasion, however, all was well, and we arrived at his spacious office where we were given coffee by his numerous personal staff. He kept getting up and peering out

The 'CINC' as the Guard of Honour marches past him.

139

of the window, which surprised me, but at length he announced, 'OK. The guys are ready and visibility is good. Let's go!' Out we went, and there in the gathering light were not only a band and Honor Guard but the whole of his staff, who must have been standing there for some time in the dark!

When it was *his* turn to visit *me*, he flew in by helicopter at the more civilised hour of 11.15. At lunch I remarked to him that I was planning a visit shortly to the States and that I was including in the itinerary a trip to Yorktown.

'You must be crazy,' he commented. 'What do you want to go there for? That's where you surrendered to George Washington.'

'I know that,' I replied. 'What's more, my own Regiment was there and surrendered too.'

'Well, I think you're crazy!'

'Oh, I don't know. Tell me: what did you think of that Honor Guard we laid on for you?'

'Very fine,' he replied.

'And what did you think of that tune the band played as they marched past you?'

'Very good; a catchy little tune.'

'Right! What you did *not* know is that *that* Honor Guard came from the Regiment that burnt down the White House, and when they had got the fire going, they marched away playing that tune!'

He liked that, and we remain firm friends to this day!

A MEMORABLE REPLY

A TV documentary about the Royal Family was produced some years ago, and it included the reception in audience of the newly appointed United States Ambassador to present his credentials. Asked how he was settling in, he replied,

'We are in the ambassadorial residence subject, of course, to some of the discomfiture as a result of the need for elements of refurbishment and rehabilitation.'

HOW TO HANDLE A TRICKY QUESTION

I was on a long and exhausting lecture tour in the States. The last question put to me at the close of the final talk was this: 'What is your government's long-term policy for the future of the Malvinas?'

I pride myself that, quick as a flash, I came back: 'Would you describe yourself as a religious man?' Yes, he would. 'Don't think me inquisitive, but are you by chance a Roman Catholic?' Yes, he was. 'Right,' I said, 'last month my wife and I were in Rome and we visited the Vatican. We were given a private tour of the Pope's apartments. Just before we entered His Holiness's library, I noticed on the wall in the passage a map of the world. I stopped, put on my spectacles and ran my eye down the Atlantic, stopping at a group of islands off the coast of South Argentina. And there, on the Pope's map, quite clearly were written the words "FALKLAND ISLANDS"!'

'Right, sir,' said my questioner. 'I withdraw that question.'

It was lucky he wasn't a Buddhist!

US MILITARY INTELLIGENCE

We enjoyed a special relationship with the Intelligence Community of the United States, and I was involved in many visits to that country, one of which took me to Fort Huachuca, Arizona, the US Army Intel School, and was instructive and entertaining. I was given a four-star stetson at a dinner in the Commandant's quarters, and towards the end of a farewell lunch in the club I was handed a note by his pretty female aide, which read:

A distinguished British General named Gow
Flew in to Huachuca somehow.
Though his humor was frightful,
We found him delightful
But it's time to depart—RIGHT NOW!

Years later when I was on duty as an Elder of the Canongate Church in Edinburgh's Royal Mile, welcoming visitors and encouraging them to look round, I encountered an American—a tourist, I discovered, from Arizona.

'I bet you've never been to Huachuca,' I said. 'I have.'

'Well goddam me!' he exclaimed, 'I was there in the Intel.' And he proceeded to tell me the following tale:

He had been given the assignment of thinking up simple and secret means of causing confusion to the enemy. His gruesome plan was to attach small incendiary devices to bats which would be directed somehow to the desired target, causing serious conflagration on arrival. Sensibly, he thought that a trial should be conducted to see whether the payload would allow the unfortunate bats to 'lift off', and accordingly his team took them in some quantity into the Arizona desert. There they were kitted out and loosed off. 'But gee, sir, there was just one thing we had overlooked. Those bats flew straight back to Huachuca, landed and started a mighty fierce blaze!'

How far he got in his military profession thereafter he never told me!

FORMAL DINING IN

My US friends and colleagues were extremely generous and kind. I was once invited to a formal military dinner in Germany, and I was given, in advance, a booklet which said in the foreword: 'This booklet is a guide in an area that offers limitless opportunity to promulgate tradition and improve morale and *esprit de corps*.'

The rules and procedures set out were comprehensive, and I was nervous that I might unwittingly commit an infringement. The following is but one passage that I studied before I attended the dinner:

A designated junior officer from each spur of the table will sample each container of wine before it is served and will place his initials on the label with a grease pencil. The failure of the junior officer to place his initials on the wine label prior to serving said bottle is in violation of proper mess procedure and will be subject to a fine as designated by Mr President. Anyone drinking wine (not champagne) from a container which has not been sampled is also in violation of the proper mess procedure. Further, anyone placing a container of/for wine (full or empty) on the table will be fined as prescribed by Mr President . . . All mess violations will be reported to Mr Vice who will then report such violations to Mr President. Normal fines will be levied in dollar increments and as determined by Mr President. Fines will be immediately collected by the designated junior warrant officer. Any participant on dining in who fails to report a violation of the rules established by the Dining-In Committee, and as approved herein, will be subjected to a fine in accordance with the principles of fines as outlined herein.

And what worried me was that I had no money on me at all!

OUR GERMAN FRIENDS

I always regretted that I never visited Berlin before the War, but my brother and I were taken by an enlightened mother, when I was eleven, to Nuremberg when the Nazi Party Rally was taking place—an experience that I shall never forget. After the War, as a soldier, I and my family spent many years in West Germany, where we made lots of friends. I have recorded some random recollections about them and their beautiful country.

OTTO, PRINCE VON BISMARCK

Queen Victoria met Otto, Prince von Bismarck, on 25 April, 1888. According to Arthur Bigge, later Lord Stamfordham, the Queen's Private Secretary, 'He came out of the room mopping his brow and said, "That was a woman. One could do business with her!"' Mrs Thatcher used almost the same words on BBC TV on 17 December, 1984: 'I like Mr Gorbachev. We could do business together.'

The only difference was that Mrs Thatcher was certainly not mopping her brow (though Mr Gorbachev might have been!)

A SENSE OF HUMOUR

If you go to the Rhineland in the spring, 'fun time' is in full swing. It is Carnival, when the Germans take their fun extremely seriously. I was reminded, when I watched some of them in action, wearing their Carnival kit, of the German Commandant of a camp for British officer prisoners of war. He too took his job seriously, and went to great trouble to learn English. Came the moment when he decided to address his inmates, and he said, 'Now you gentlemen think I know damn nothing about this subject, but before I have done, you will see that I know damn all!'

The Germans take their fun very seriously. Carnival time in the Rhineland.

BERLIN, 1945

Shortly after the War ended, I went up to Berlin as a staff officer in the Control Commission, which at that time was working harmoniously with our American and French allies, but less so with the Russians. When I arrived, my boss told me that I would actually be his ADC (to which, as a brigadier, he was not entitled—but never mind). My job would be to ensure that his house in the Grünewald was the best in the whole of that devastated city. He would be doing a great deal of entertaining in competition with our allies, and for the sake of British prestige, *we* had to be 'the tops'.

145

This challenge was just up my street, and, as an energetic young captain, I set to work. The central heating was renovated, the garage repaired and the cellar suitably stocked. I found and engaged as butler a German who claimed to have been a servant to King George V at the Delhi Durbar (and he looked the part!). He in turn engaged a bevy of maids, all of whom seemed to me to have been selected for their good looks; they knew the form, however, as they had themselves been mistresses, in better times, of households employing considerable staffs.

It was therefore hardly surprising that when I eventually completed my tour of duty I departed with a glowing report from my charming boss, and we remain close friends to this day.

Number 25 Messel Strasse in the Grünewald district of Berlin, which, when most of the rest of the city was devastated, had remained reasonably untouched. In November 1945 I was instructed to ensure that it was the best residence occupied by any of the Allies—and I did!

146

THE 'KURDAMM'

In 1945 the Kurfürstendamm, like most of Berlin, was in ruins. One evening a friend invited me to accompany him out to dinner in this famous thoroughfare, which was now merely a narrow pathway through the rubble and, of course, completely unlit. He took me to what quite clearly was a totally bombed and gutted building, and I remember thinking that he was either mad or had got lost. Not at all: he knocked at the still intact door and we descended to the basement, entering a very sophisticated restaurant, candle-lit, to the music of a splendid dance band, and there we enjoyed a memorable meal.

That was 45 years ago. *Der Berliner Morgenpost* of Sunday 5 June, 1983, published the following about an event in the same street:

Right to the last minute the grandiose spectacle remains 'top secret'. It is Friday evening, the time 7 pm. The Kurfürstendamm is seething with people. Berlin is on the move. The police seal off the entrance to number 37. As quick as a flash a row of illegally parked cars is towed away out of the prohibited zone—there is a huge gathering of people. The curious ask, 'What's going on here, then?', but no one will tell. 'Inconspicuous' German and British security officials seal off the entrance to the rear courtyard of the Alt-Berliner Schneckenhaus. A red carpet is rolled out. Only those who can prove their identity with an invitation are allowed to pass . . . Now the rhythmic beat starts, with drum rolls and fanfares. Black limousines drive up. Sixty British guests of honour, amongst them the highest-ranking generals of Her Majesty Queen Elizabeth II, wearing dinner-jackets, are gathering with their wives in evening dresses, for an extraordinary Berlin dinner. The reason: a triple birthday. 'Just for Fun.' The Commander-in-Chief of the British Army of the Rhine is celebrating his 59th birthday; on his arm is his pretty blonde daughter, Belinda, who lives in Rome and is 25 years old today. The proprietor of the Alt-Berliner Schneckenhaus, Helmut Gaber, has invited them both and their guests to *his* 48th birthday celebration . . . The British Chief had held his 35th wedding anniversary party a year ago at the Berliner's restaurant. 'Your Excellency,' the proprietor had promised at the time, 'let's celebrate together next year . . .' 'Excellent,' smiled the General with delight, and so right now he was moving in with five dozen of his best friends from London and West Germany.

Berlin as I first knew it, in 1945, when I visited the restaurant in the Kurdamm. *Photo: by permission of the Imperial War Museum*

And the article concluded:

The finale took place in the early hours of Saturday on the Kurfürstendamm. Three pipers from the Scottish Highlands, three Scots Guards from General Gow's own regiment, play Scottish airs, and close, as the sun rises over Berlin, with the Scottish National Anthem; the grandiose spectacle is over!

All I can say is that times certainly change!

The triple birthday party—my daughter's 25th, my 59th and Herr Gaber's 48th.

KAISER WILHELM II

In my experience, officers of the German General Staff are extremely efficient, and the military staff of His Imperial Majesty must have been specially selected and therefore ultra-efficient, as evidenced by the following anecdote:

While I have always found it difficult to remember names, faces and places, not so the Kaiser—or so it seemed. During a military inspection at Potsdam in the 1900s, it is said, while riding down the ranks he suddenly stopped and, pointing to a soldier in the centre rank, exclaimed, 'Ah, Schmidt! I remember you! I saw you on parade in Dresden—now let me think—five years ago, and I seem to recall that Frau Schmidt was about to have her fourth child. Please give her my regards.'

149

Not unnaturally, this created a great impression on the troops (and particularly on Schmidt!), but it was not in fact due to the Kaiser being blessed with a fantastic memory. For he held on the pommel of his saddle a brief: 'Count 16. Centre rank. Moustache. Schmidt. Dresden 5 years ago. Frau S 4th child on way'.

All was well, provided H.I.M. could count!

SOVEREIGNTY!

The day when West Germany was to be granted sovereignty by the Allies, who would then cease to be the occupying powers, was announced several weeks in advance. Every soldier of every rank was briefed in detail on the implications, and instructed to pass on the information to their wives and families.

I recall attending such a briefing for senior commanders and staff officers, given by a rather deaf retired Major General. I took in every word, and even made a note or two. I then briefed my wife, explaining that on a certain Thursday *we* would no longer be in charge, as it were, and would all be subject to German civil law. We would, in short, be equals.

One day when I returned home she told me that she had noticed a marked change in the attitude of Germans in the shops to her.

'Why is that, do you think?' I asked.

'That's good, I must say,' she retorted, 'coming from you. It's Thursday today; you know, sovereignty and all that!'

'No! No! It's not this Thursday; *next* one is *der Tag*!'

I don't think she believed me, but it was so.

*   *   *

150

I remember another occasion when I had to arrange an Old Wykehamist dinner in Germany, at which the same Major General, himself an Old Wykehamist, was to preside because of his age and seniority. We gathered for this meal, and while we were having pre-prandial drinks I looked round at the assembled company and thought they looked simply awful—deadly serious and earnest—and felt it my duty to liven things up a bit. So I told the bandmaster that when dinner was announced and as we trooped in, he was to play the 'Eton Boating Song', which he did.

The old General was absolutely furious, and never spoke to me again!

HITLER'S ADC

I was invited to lunch in a beautiful flat in Düsseldorf where a former officer of the Waffen SS lived with his Swedish wife. His name was Schulze Cossens and he had written two books about his Nazi organisation, copies of which he signed and gave me with pride. After lunch he invited me into his study, which in fact was the entire flat on the floor above, identical except that there was no bathroom or kitchen. It was full of books, documents, archives and photographs of the Hitler period, and I noticed one photo that showed him with Ribbentrop and Molotov. He told me that it was taken in Moscow in 1939, when, as Ribbentrop's aide, he had accompanied him there when the Russo-German Agreement was signed. He had then been appointed the Waffen SS ADC to the Führer until 1944.

This had been the highlight of his whole life, and when he spoke to me of Hitler, his face was transformed. ('Of course I get a good pension as an officer in the SS. Do you know, if I had been in the Gestapo, I wouldn't get one at all! Don't you think that's wrong?') I asked him if he had been on Hitler's staff in July 1944, when the assassination attempt had taken place. He told me that he had, and that he had been with the Führer at the fatal conference.

'How did you survive?' I inquired.

'Well, it was a pretty boring meeting, and I wanted to go to the loo, so I slipped out for a moment—and that was the precise moment when the bomb went off.'

'That must have been a bit awkward for you.'

'Yes, it was,' he admitted—and I now cannot recall just how he got out of his predicament.

He could talk of nothing else but those glorious days, and when I asked if he would like to appear in a TV interview in England, he was thrilled. An eminent interviewer visited him, but in the event nothing came of it. 'All he could talk about was Hitler,' complained the interviewer—'Hopeless.'

But that, I thought, was the whole point!

MONTE CASSINO

In the chapel of the monastery at Monte Cassino I came across a singular man. He was a professor at Würzburg University, and we sat side by side during the service. When we left the chapel he introduced himself as von der Heide, remarking, 'I've only been here once before, you know.'

'When was that?' I asked.

'I was ordered to do a reconnaissance of a defensive line here in the War, and I came to the monastery, heard the monks singing and went in to listen. Afterwards I lunched with the Abbot, and I've never been back till now.'

He was an interesting man who had seen action in almost every campaign and battle of which I had heard. He told me that he personally had invented novel tactics for 'taking out' British anti-aircraft guns in Malta, by a combination of Stuka dive-bomber strikes and gliders that were trained to land on target shortly after the air attack. Trials of this technique had been successfully carried out by a female pilot whose prowess was greatly admired by Hitler, and the only reason why the operation never took place was because Mussolini had insisted that it must be under Italian command and control—which, of course, would have meant total failure,' he said.

Von der Heide also told me that he had commanded Rommel's rearguard after Alamein, effectively delaying the British follow-up with soup plates, which were consistently mistaken for anti-tank mines. He related that one evening he was sitting in his tent when he heard an English voice calling, 'Hello! Hello! Anyone there?', to which he replied, 'Yes! Come along here!'

Into his tent stepped a young British cavalry officer, who asked, 'I say, do you happen to know where we are?'

'Yes, I think so,' replied von der Heide, and showed him the map.

'Thanks a lot,' said the officer, and then stopped, gazing at his helper. 'I say. Aren't you a German?'

'That's right.'

'What rank are you?'

'I'm a major.'

'Gosh. I'm only a captain so I suppose I'm your prisoner.'

'I'm afraid so,' said the German, 'but never mind. Have a glass of whisky. It's good—it should be; it's some of yours I made prisoner too!'

A GENERAL AND A CASSINO VETERAN

In my last field appointment, my superior officer was a man of very great military, intellectual and artistic distinction. He had been wounded several times in the War and lost an arm, and had survived the disaster of Stalingrad in the nick of time. He and his wife came to stay with us in London and we took them to church in the chapel of the Royal Hospital, Chelsea, after which we were invited to accompany the governor on his 'rounds' of one of the companies.

General 'Deidi' von Senger und Etterlin, Commander-in-Chief Central Region of NATO (CINCERT) with myself, Commander Northern Army Group (COMNORTHAG).

The in-Pensioners were standing to attention at the entrances to their little bunks, and I said to my friend, 'Look at this chap's medal ribbons. *That* one is the Italy star'; and he asked the veteran where he had served.

'Monte Cassino,' came the reply.

'Oh,' said my friend, 'how interesting. My father was there.'

'Perhaps I met the gentleman,' said the Pensioner. 'What was his name, sir?'

To which the reply was: 'No. I doubt whether you would have met. *My* name is General von Senger und Etterlin, the same as my father's, and *he* was commanding the German Corps opposite you.'

And the funny thing was that the veteran seemed neither surprised nor particularly impressed!

SAVED FROM CERTAIN DEATH

It was rare to come across any German officer who admitted that he had fought on the Western Front, so I was, I thought on pretty safe ground when on one occasion during dinner I said to one of the staff officers in my international headquarters, 'I suppose you were in the thrust against Moscow?'

'Yes.'

'And I expect that you were commanding an armoured platoon at the very tip of the Schwerpunkt?'

'Certainly.'

'And I suppose you actually came within sight of the Kremlin?'

'Oh, yes.'

'Well how is it that you are sitting beside me now? You should surely be dead?'

His reply was interesting: he claimed that as evening fell he had said to his soldiers that they would pause for rest, restock with fuel and ammunition, then move on at first light the next day, and they would be in Moscow.

There had, however, always been a law or custom, so he said, that the eldest son of an aristocratic family (such as he was) was not allowed to be at duty in action (as he was). Quite by chance his mother had discovered what he was up

155

to and had complained to the military authorities. As a result, when dawn broke, instead of leading the advance to Moscow, he was ordered to be withdrawn to an administrative post in the rear areas, and *that* was how it had come about that he was sitting next to me at dinner that night!

A NIGHT AT AN EMBASSY ABROAD

When I was staying with an ambassadorial friend in the American capital, I remarked that I was about to visit a southern European capital to lecture and that I was going to be put up there by his colleague, whom I had not previously met. 'He's a very erudite fellow,' my friend said, 'and I think, though I'm not absolutely sure, a classical scholar of some note.'

Mindful of this, I went bearing a gift that I thought would be appreciated: my uncle Andrew Gow's edition of Theocritus—a weighty tome if ever there was one. I had even written the Ambassador's name within, adding the date and 'd.d. JMG', which I thought might indicate that I was a kindred spirit. As I presented it, I was tempted to quote the immortal line of Virgil's *Aeneid*, *'Timeo Danaos et dona ferentes'*—'I fear the Danaans, even when they bring gifts', but I thought I might be over-egging it.

When, however, His Excellency opened the present, from his face it was quite plain that he did not understand a single word of the text; I might just as well have given him a book in Tibetan!

I was told that I had been invited out to dinner and that when I got back HE and his wife would have gone to bed. 'Don't forget to lock up and turn the light off when you return,' I was asked, and in due course, after an enjoyable evening I returned, remembering to do as I had been told. I mounted the magnificent staircase, and found passages branching off from the landing in all directions. Heavens! I simply could not remember where my bedroom was! No one was about and I tip-toed round, opening doors and peering in. I'd never seen so many bedrooms in my life. I went into one: a shaft of moonlight fell across a bed—Their Excellencies slumbering! Out I crept to continue my search, and then panic seized me: I could not remember which rooms I had looked in! More and more doors I opened; Gracious! The ambassadorial room again!

What made it all the more alarming was that where normally one would have expected to find a light switch, instead there was a bell, which I kept ringing! At length, utterly exhausted, I decided that I simply *must* lie down somewhere; maybe in the morning a servant would rescue me. I stood in the passage and offered up a prayer of despair before I entered what had to be a haven of rest. My prayer was answered: it *was* my room!

Next morning, or rather a few hours later, the Ambassadress greeted me at breakfast. Had I slept well?

'Like a top,' said the liar.

'I do hope you weren't disturbed in the night,' she remarked. 'A bell kept ringing intermittently. I must have the telephone checked.'

'No, I heard nothing,' I assured her.

What a night!

15
Final Appointment

When I completed my tour as Commander-in-Chief in Germany I was nearly 60 and, in the opinion of my family, 'getting a bit past it, don't you think?' Nevertheless, I was given further and most welcome employment for another two years as Commandant of the Royal College of Defence Studies in Belgrave Square , where we lived in a mews flat. I could not think of a nicer way to complete my active life in the service of the Sovereign.

A SIGNAL

From: General Sir John Stanier, Chief of the
General Staff
To: General Sir Michael Gow

For Commandant from CGS. I am reminded of
your signal to me on the occasion of my
Regiment's Waterloo Dinner last May. May I
reciprocate by welcoming you most warmly to
the RCDS and by saying how glad I am that you
too are now 'surrounded by bright intelligent
faces': indeed some might say 'at last'!

The Chief was Colonel of the Royal Scots Dragoon Guards, and his regiment each year marked the gallant action of the Greys against the French at Waterloo in 1815 by a special dinner. I must presumably have made some complimentary comment in my signal to him on that occasion about the brain-power of his officers.

Naturally I replied by letter, on the second day of taking up my post:

Sir,

I was, as always, deeply moved by your signalled communication which greeted me as I assumed my appointment here yesterday. I have, for many years, been encouraged, as I walk down the path of life, by the trust and confidence which you have displayed in me, and when I address the Members here this morning, I shall leave them in no doubt that the entire college syllabus is designed, like some Wagnerian score, to reach the fortissimo crescendo marked by your own Address here. Until then, the general welfare of the Members, the Directing Staff, Administrators and, primarily, of the Commandant, will be at the forefront of my mind.

        I have the honour to remain,
        Sir,
        Your obedient Servant,

        Michael Law
        General

16
Military Miscellany

ARMY CATERING

Food is—and always has been, for good or ill—a matter of importance in the Army. It is referred to sometimes as 'scoff', after, I deduce, the famous French chef M. Escoffier, who was sent out to the seat of war in the Crimea to improve the deplorable food being issued to the troops.

At the periodical welfare meetings which are held in regiments and battalions, attended by squadron or company representatives, 'messing' is always discussed and any complaints noted. A famous Irish Guards Quartermaster, Major Keatinge, was once presiding at one of these at Pirbright, when one of the 'reps' put up his hand.

'Yes?'

'Sir, why can't we have butter on our bread at breakfast and not marg?'

'Are you a religious man?' he was asked.

'Yes, sir.'

'Well, stand up and recite the Lord's Prayer.'

And the Guardsman started off, 'Our Father which art in heaven . . . Give us this day our daily bread . . .'

'Stop!' shouted the QM. 'Did God say anything about butter? No, so sit down and be quiet!'

Once, when I was appointed Catering Officer at Pirbright,

the Adjutant told me that I would have to attend a course at Aldershot to learn all about calories and so on. Unfortunately, on arrival, to my surprise I found that I had been sent on a cookery course by mistake— and, if my memory is right, a long one at that. Week 1 was devoted to soups, and as a result, although I say it myself, I became quite a 'dab hand'. (I recently made several gallons for a congregational lunch in the manse of the Kirk of which I am an Elder, and it was reported that one old wifey thought it so delicious that she had four helpings!)

Week 2 was all about the 'haversack ration', which ordinary folk call 'sandwiches', and so important was this subject rated that an officer came all the way down from London to lecture about it. We assembled in a lecture hall marked by a plaque commemorating Sir Isadore Salmon, founder of the Army Catering Corps. When the lights dimmed, a 'spot' fell upon our visitor. He spoke at length, and the keensters on the course took notes. 'We will now put on a little playlet,' he announced, 'to show you the WRONG way of making the haversack ration' (and my neighbour wrote down 'WRONG WAY' and underlined it, just to make sure).

The curtains parted on the stage to reveal a mock-up of a railway compartment, in which were sitting some pretty army girls in uniform. The door suddenly opened and in stepped the scruffiest soldier imaginable. He threw his haversack into the rack and started to read a comic. A whistle blast was heard, and by the jolting of the passengers, assisted by noises off, it was clear that the train had started. After a while the soldier looked at his watch: 'scoff time,' he clearly thought. He got down his haversack and, with all the girls watching, extracted a packet wrapped in newspaper which he slowly opened to reveal two hunks of bread with a lump of cheese in the middle. As the curtains closed, all the girls were tittering and the soldier was overcome with embarrassment.

162

'Right, then,' said the lecturer, 'that was the WRONG way. Now we will demonstrate the RIGHT way.' And again my neighbour made a note. The scene was the same, but this time the soldier was immaculate—an Adonis. The girls were agog, especially when he took down his haversack. Slowly he opened the contents, revealing wafer-thin sandwiches, with crusts removed, and individually wrapped in 'cling film'. As the curtains closed, he was offering them round to the girls, who were giving him their telephone numbers!

'Never forget,' we were exhorted, 'the sandwich must be not only palatable to the tongue but also *pleasing to the eye*'—and I never have!

A COLONEL VISITS HIS REGIMENT

The late Major General Sir 'Jackie' d'Avigdor-Goldsmid, Colonel of his old regiment, was coming over to Germany to pay them a visit. As he was an old friend and godfather to one of my daughters, I invited him to spend a night with us on the way.

I asked him what he actually did on these visits. He told me in some detail . . . and added that on one evening he was always entertained in the sergeants' mess.

'That must be fun,' I remarked. 'You meet all your old chums, don't you?'

'The trouble is,' he replied, 'that I'm so old that all my old chums have left the Regiment.'

'I'm sure, though, that as the evening wears on some ancient sergeant will fix his beady eyes upon you and with great concentration and care walk across and put his arm on your shoulder, saying, 'I remember you, sir. The best bloody officer we've ever had!'

'It's funny you should say that', he replied. 'On my last visit the scene that you have described did take place, but the 'ancient sergeant', as you called him, said, 'I remember you, sir. You were the *worst* bloody adjutant we've ever had!'

A CHARACTER DEFECT

In the aftermath of Burgess, Vassall, Maclean *et al.*, a system of vetting was introduced into the armed forces and other departments of government. There were two grades: lesser mortals were subjected to 'negative vetting' (NV), while those in positions of greater import were 'positively vetted' (PV'd). It was a bit of a status symbol to be PV'd, and the process involved considerable research into background, habits and 'character defects'. Discovery of one of these last could be pretty damning, and could bring a halt to an otherwise promising career if not voluntarily divulged. Mine, fortunately never became known to the security authorities, and it is only now, years after retirement, that I feel able to *reveal all* for the first time!

My wife and I were once invited out to lunch by people whom we hardly knew, and I found myself seated next to a large lady whom I had never met and who had a mass of blonde, bouffant hair.

While I was chatting away, making rather heavy weather of both the conversation and the steak, my knife and fork slipped, depositing meat and two veg. upon my neighbour. Overcome with embarrassment, I apologised profusely and, evidently quite inadequately, did my best to repair the damage. A few moments later when I turned in an attempt to resume our somewhat frigid relationship, I espied, nestling in her fair locks, a piece of mashed potato! I was horrified, and desperately wondered what I should do. The conclusion to which I came was to do nothing, and for the rest of the meal there the spud remained.

My wife and I fled the house before the coffee. When she asked me why we had hurried off, and I told her, she merely said that I was lacking in moral courage—a sure character defect!

'It's the Foreign Office—they want to know whether you can possibly remember that frightfully funny story you told them at the time of Burgess and Maclean?' Cartoon by Osbert Lancaster. *Reproduced by permission of the Estate of Sir Osbert lancaster and John Murray (Publishers) Ltd*

NON-OFFICER STATUS

Had the event that I have just described been detected and evaluated earlier in my life, I might well never have been accepted for a commission in the Army.

'Now, let's just think,' remarked one of my children. 'Just suppose you had never risen higher than, let's say, a lance corporal, what suitable employment could have been found for you in the Scots Guards?' And they all made suggestions: Commanding Officer's staff car driver? No; he doesn't like being kept up late. Company storeman? Weak at accounting. Sergeant major's batman? Not a lance corporal post, and anyhow he's not too good at polishing boots.

At long last the conclusion was that there was only one possible job, and it would be in the rank of Guardsman: officers' mess silver man—and *that* simply because they thought the Regiment hadn't much silver to be kept clean!

CIVILIAN EMPLOYMENT

The following letter was despatched by a staff officer at the Army Headquarters, Scotland:

```
DCOS/32

15 Mar 89

Dist Sec

EMPLOYMENT—CRAIGIEHALL

1.  I was approached during the Laying Up of
the Old Colours of the Second Battalion Scots
Guards on Tuesday by a former Scots Guardsman
```

who was wondering if there were any vacancies
for Messengers/Security Guards at Craigiehall.
I said I would try and find out.

2. The man in question is J.M. Gow. He lives
in Edinburgh and is, in fact, over 65 but is
active and seeking further employment. I
wonder if your CM staff can be of assistance.

J.A. DUNSMURE
Colonel
DCOS

I was too old!—Alas, the request was turned down.

A COMMANDING OFFICER'S INSPECTION

The Commanding Officer at Gordon Barracks, Aberdeen,
was an officer in the Black Watch, renowned for their
splendid history and traditions, and for the red hackle
which they wore in their bonnets—a unique mark of
distinction.

During an inspection of the rooms of the junior pipers, he
decided to examine the contents of the lockers, and chose
one belonging to a Gordon Highlander. Behind a pair of
neatly folded socks he found an extremely fine hackle,
measuring some five inches.

'What's this, for goodness' sake?'

The piper replied that it was a red hackle.

'I know perfectly well *what* it is,' retorted the CO, 'but
what are *you*, a junior piper in the Gordons, doing with it?'

167

And to this the soldier replied, 'Ah weel, sirr, ah just use it for tae dust ma locker oot wi', ye ken'!

THE ART OF COMMAND

General (later Field Marshal the Viscount) Slim was a very charismatic leader, and his addresses to the troops under his command were impressive. Before one offensive by his Army in Burma, he addressed a battalion whose role would be crucial to the success of the operation. It is said that he greatly stirred his audience. Indeed, one sergeant was so carried away that he shouted out, 'Rely on us! We'll be right behind you, sir!'

'You bloody well won't,' replied Slim, 'I'll be a hundred miles behind *you*!'

LONDON CLUBS

Clubs are popular with the military, and when I was posted to London my son said to me, 'You haven't got a club, have you?' You really should, you know. I'll put you up for mine.'

'I hope it's not costly?' I enquired.

'Oh no,' he assured me, and suggested that I should meet him there one day, the following week, for a drink at 6 pm.

Accordingly I was there, as a good Scots Guardsman is wont, seven minutes before the stated time, and enquired of the hall porter whether my son had arrived. The porter seemed vague but suggested that I should wait in the smoking-room, which I did. Time passed and I began to get bored so I wandered into the hall and read some of the notices on the board. 'That's funny,' I thought. 'I wonder why the Travellers' Club has so many things up about the

Reform.' And then it dawned on me that I was in fact in the wrong club! 'Why are you late?' asked my son when I moved to the correct establishment next door, but I didn't let on.

'Steady on with the untreated effluent, Mousehole!' Cartoon by Osbert Lancaster. *Reproduced by permission of the Estate of Sir Osbert Lancaster and John Murray (Publishers) Ltd*

Sometime later I got a letter from the secretary of the club for which my son had put me up, saying that I had been elected. Would I please send a cheque for £400 entrance and first year's subscription? When I next saw my son, I complained bitterly: 'I thought you said it wasn't expensive. Just look at what I've had to fork out!'

'Well,' he said, '*I* didn't have to pay that.'

'I'm not interested in what *you* had to pay.'

'Why don't you resign, then?' he suggested.

'Don't be silly. I've only just been elected, and if I did, I should go in the Guinness Book of Records for having bought the most expensive glass of gin and tonic ever—costing £400.75!'

*　　*　　*

A military friend recalled the following club anecdotes, which I consider worth recording:

'I was in the Turf Club on day [during the War] just after the end of a bad bombing time, when an old member tottered in on two sticks, rang the bell, and when the waiter appeared bellowed to him, "Find the 1898 volume of the Bloodstock Breeder!" The waiter accepted the order as quite normal, and to my surprise shortly produced it.'

'A somewhat deaf member of the club, during a severe blitz, rang the bell and said to the old waiter, "Tell those fellers upstairs to stop makin' that infernal row!"'

BADGES OF RANK

Unlike the Chinese army of Chairman Mao, the British have been keen, generally speaking, on displaying badges of rank, and it has often struck some as odd that those of a brigadier should be so ornate—a crown surmounting three stars, set in a triangle. Before the invention of the 'Staybrite' technique, a considerable amount of polishing was required to maintain them in pristine condition.

Once, as a brigadier, I went to work with one of the stars missing, and this omission was pointed out to me by everyone I met, except for those who were so small that they could see no higher than my chest.

At length, exasperated, I said, 'I'm surprised that you don't know. Today is the anniversary of the battle of Inkerman in which the Scots Guards fought with distinction. The Commanding Officer was severely wounded in the right shoulder but he carried on pluckily, felling Russians with his sword arm, despite the agony he was enduring. The Prince Consort, Colonel of the Regiment, directed that this gallantry should never be forgotten and decreed that on Inkerman Day for all time officers of the Regiment would deliberately shed one star from their right shoulder.'

'Oh of course,' said my questioner, 'I should have remembered. We were told all about it at Sandhurst. I do apologise.'

I naturally did not tell him that I had invented this tear-jerking tale that very moment!

A GAME OF SQUASH

During a tour at the Joint Headquarters at Rheindahlen in West Germany, as it was then called, I was driven by a charming WRAC corporal. One day she asked me if I had ever played squash, and I revealed to her that in my younger days I had played a lot and had been pretty good. I asked her if she played, to which the answer was that she did. 'Would you like to have a game with me?' she asked. Although I was not up to my former standard, I told her, I would be delighted to. She said that she would book the court for the following day at 6 pm, adding that she happened to be playing that very evening if I cared to drop in.

As I had nothing else to do, I did drop in, and to my astonishment there she was in a fantastic outfit, complete with a blazer covered in badges. She was the WRAC squash champion!

Next morning, when she was driving me to work, I said, 'Look here! I haven't got the kind of smart sports kit that you've got, and I couldn't possibly play you in my old grey flannel trousers.'

'No problem, sir,' she said. 'I'll pop into the NAAFI stores and get you a pair of white shorts.'

I thought that I was on to a safe bet because she would never be able to get a pair to fit me, but she did (just!), and accordingly at five minutes to six I arrived at the court, where I heard her knocking up. I entered, and as I shut the court door I happened to glance up at the balcony—which was packed with members of the WRAC!

Readers of this anecdote will now expect me to relate what happened, but they will be disappointed! They will deduce that I am either very modest or very embarrassed—and I will not reveal which!

17
Tales of the Kirk

AN ENGLISH SERMON

I recall an old Church of England minister getting into the pulpit at matins, preparatory to delivering his sermon, while the first verse of the rather long preceding hymn was being sung. At its conclusion, we sat down and the cleric said, 'You may have wondered why I entered the pulpit today somewhat earlier than usual. I thought it might help me to remember what I was going to talk to you about, but it hasn't! So I think we had better go on with the next hymn!'

METHODS OF DELIVERY

Dean Ramsay relates the following:

To a minister who used a manuscript in delivering his address, a member of the congregation remarked, 'What gars ye tak your bit papers to the pulpit?' The reply was that he could not remember his sermon and so must have them.

'Weel, weel, Minister,' commented the questioner, 'then dinna expect that *we* can remember them.'

'Now, Runcible, let us see whether this year we can't get right through "Adeste Fideles" without my having to speak to anyone about hogging the mike.' Cartoon by Osbert Lancaster. *Reproduced by permission of the Estate of Sir Osbert Lancaster and John Murray (Publishers) Ltd*

A CLERICAL INTRODUCTION

It is said that the great hostess Mrs Ronnie Greville once addressed the poet John Drinkwater as 'Mr Bayswater'.

'My name is not "Bayswater", he remarked.

'I'm so sorry, Mr Bathwater,' she apologised.

*　　　*　　　*

The late and famous Reverend Lawrence Matthews, once Chaplain to the Household Division and a great character, wished to present an assistant padre, the Reverend Rex Hancock, to a Royal Personage who was attending a service at the Guards Chapel. 'Your Royal Highness, may I present the Reverend Tony Hancock? No, that's not right! I mean, of course, the Reverend Rex Harrison!'

MISTAKEN IDENTITY?

The minister of Kelso drew my attention to a report in the local newspaper—with, I should add, a touch of jealousy. It read: 'The Royal British Legion Scotland is gathering for their annual conference in Kelso under their President, General God.'

*　　　*　　　*

I was once asked to give an address at Winchester College, and found that I was an alternative to attending Sunday Chapel. I was incensed to see so many boys present: 'I must tell you all that I strongly object to any of you being here! You should not be here to listen to GOW, but in there' (pointing to chapel) 'listening to GOD!'

A HIGHLAND MINISTER

A Highland minister once chose as his text, 'He gathered His children unto him as a hen gathers her chicks beneath her wings'; and this he repeated, so that his congregation would have it clear in their minds. I thought that with a bit of

175

imagination he might be able to sustain an address based on that text for a maximum of ten minutes, but when I looked at my watch and found that he had been going for twice that length of time, with no apparent prospect of conclusion, I sat up, intrigued to see how he was achieving what I had thought to be impossible.

His technique was in fact simple: at the end of each phase of the address, he repeated his text and said again in the next phase what he had already said, but using slightly different words. He drew stumps after 40 minutes, and shook me warmly by the hand as I left, recognising as he did so that I was a stranger.

'An' whit did ye think o' my woords?' he enquired.

'Minister,' I truthfully replied, 'they have left an indelible mark on my mind'—and they had!

A TALE OF A VERGER

My parents were married in the Chapel of King Henry VII in Westminster Abbey, which was being restored after war damage when my own wedding was held, so that our ceremony took place in the nave. On both occasions a senior verger, Brown, who had been an old friend of my grandfather, Dr James Gow, was on duty and processed ahead of the married couples.

I got to know him well and used to visit him for a chat whenever I happened to be in London. One such occasion was in the year of the coronation of our Queen. I remarked that I assumed he would be assigned some position of importance in the proceedings, and he agreed that this would be so. Later I asked him what he had actually done.

'Oh, sir,' he exclaimed, 'I don't think I'll ever recover from it!'

'I'm so pleased that it has been such a high spot in your

life here.'

'Not at all,' he continued. 'I couldn't believe that the authorities could do such a thing to me. I was put in charge of the peeresses' toilets!'

I fear that this may have contributed to his premature demise.

Brown, the Verger, in the cloisters of Westminster Abbey, 3 October, 1946.

A FISHING INCIDENT

Three clergymen went out fishing. Just after the boat had been pushed from the shore, the Roman Catholic priest said that he had brought the wrong rod. He promptly jumped over the side, walked over the water and picked up his correct tackle; then without a word he walked back to take his place on board. The next moment the Church of Scotland minister did the same thing. Not wishing to be outdone, their Anglican colleague said that he was going to go ashore to change his rod, and leapt upon the water—which at once swallowed him up, and he sank to the bottom.

The Roman Catholic then said to the minister, 'We really should have told him where the stepping stones are!'

The minister looked puzzled and replied, 'Oh, I didn't know there were any!'

18
Scottish Vignettes

ON SCOTLAND AND THE SCOTS

Surprise was expressed by some cattle dealers in Inverary that Nelson should have signalled at Trafalgar in the terms, 'England expects . . .'.

'Ah, Nelson only said "expects" of the English. He said nothing of Scotland for he kent the Scots would do theirs.'

*   *   *

Queen Victoria to the Crown Princess of Prussia, 10 February, 1871: 'One of the last walks I took with dear Papa, he said to me, "England does not know what she owes to Scotland." She is the brightest jewel in my crown—energy, courage, worth, inimitable perseverance, determination and self-respect.'

*   *   *

Sydney Smith (1771–1845), in Lady Holland's Memoirs: 'It requires a surgical operation to get a joke well into a Scotch understanding. Their only idea of wit . . . is laughing immoderately at stated intervals.'

*   *   *

Charles Lamb (1775–1834): 'I have been trying all my life to like Scotchmen and I am obliged to desist from the experiment in despair!'

*   *   *

George Bernard Shaw: 'God help England if she had no Scots to think for her.'

*   *   *

Sir James Barrie's rectorial address at St Andrew's, 1922: 'You come from a race of men, the very wind of whose name has swept to the ultimate seas.'

*   *   *

Scots proverb:

> The Englishman greets
> The Irishman sleeps
> But the Scotsman gangs till he gets it.

ANECDOTES COLLECTED BY DEAN RAMSAY

An English tourist, in Arran to fish, was advised that the cleg (or horse-fly) would be a good lure. He said to Kirstie, a Highland servant-girl, 'Can you get me some horse-flies?' She did not understand him, and he exclaimed, 'Why, girl, did you never see a horse-fly?'

To which she replied, 'Naa , sir, but A wance saw a coo jump over a preshipice!'

*   *   *

An Ayrshire gentleman, out on 1 September, was such a bad shot that he failed to bring down a single bird. His bag-carrier pointed out to him a large covey, thick and close on the stubble. 'Noo, Mr Jones, let drive at them just as they are.' He did, and hit not one. All flew off safely.

'Hey, sir, but ye've made those yins shift their quarters!'

*   *   *

During the examination in the House of Lords of the magistrates of Edinburgh concerning the Porteous Riot in 1736, the Duke of Newcastle asked the Provost with what kind of shot the Town Guard, which he had commanded, had loaded their muskets.

'Oh, juist sic and ane shutes dukes and sic like fules wi'.'

Luckily the Duke of Argyll was able to explain that the Provost was referring not to peers and idiots but to ducks and waterfowl.

*   *   *

At Hawick the people used to wear clogs, which made a considerable noise on the pavement. An old woman was dying, and one of the friends by her bedside said to her, 'Weel, Jenny, ye are gawn to heeven, an'gin you should see oor folk, ye can tell them that we're a' weel.'

To which she replied, 'Weel, gin I should see them I'se tell them, but ye manna expect that I'm to gang clank, clanking through heeven lookin for your folk.'

*   *   *

An old shoe-maker in Glasgow was sitting by the bedside of his wife, who was dying. She took him by the hand.

'Weel, John, we're gawin to part. I've been a gude wife to ye, John.'

'Oh just middling, just middling, Jenny.'

'John, ye maun promise to bury me in the auld kirkyard at Stra'ron, beside my mither. I couldna rest in peace among unco' folk, in the dirt and smoke o' Glasgow.'

'Weel, weel Jenny, my woman,' said John soothingly, 'we'll just pit ye in the Gorbals first, and gin ye dinna lie quiet, we'll try ye in Sta'ron.'

NIEL GOW

Niel Gow, one of my forebears (born in 1727), has been described thus: 'the supreme fiddler, with an easy manner of a Highlander, enjoying the patronage of his laird. Gow takes his place with the performers, collectors and composers of the eighteenth century—an unique breed, living in a culturally enriched environment of a rare age.' And another has said: 'Gow became, in fact, almost a national monument, thought of as being a characteristic "model of what national partiality conceives a Scottish Highlander to be".' The following anecdotes are recorded about this remarkable man:

Once when Lady Charlotte Murray sat down at the pianoforte, Niel said to her mother, the Duchess, 'that lassie o' yours, my leddie, has a guid ear.' A gentleman present said, 'I thought, Niel, you had more manners than to call Her Grace's daughter "a lassie".' To which Gow replied, 'What could I call her? I never heard she was a laddie!'—which, while it astonished the gentleman, highly amused the noble parties themselves.

*   *   *

Two pompous gentlemen were walking along a road near Dunkeld and came across a fellow-traveller. 'Are you not Niel Gow, the fiddler?' they asked, to which the cautious reply was 'Aye'.

'Then you are the very man we have come all the way from Glasgow to see.'

Niel Gow, from a portrait by Sir Henry Raeburn. *Reproduced by permission of the National Galleries of Scotland*

183

'Then you're the muir fules,' retorted Gow. 'Ah wadna' gang half as far tae see you!'

*   *   *

'Oh, Mr Gow,' remarked the Duchess of Gordon, 'I've not been at all well lately. In the mornings my head swims—a sudden giddiness comes upon me . . .' To which the musical genius replied, 'Ah ken whit ye mean, your leddyship. When I've been fu' [drunk] the nicht before it's like a hail bike [swarm] o' bees buzzin in ma bonnet.'

*   *   *

Murray of Abercairney was one of those numerous products of eighteenth-century Scottish aristocracy who retained the common touch—just the kind of man to find a kindred spirit in Gow. And many a jovial time they had together. On one occasion Abercairney gave Gow a loan of £5, on the understanding that he was to be repaid in music. Some time afterwards, at a party held in Dunkeld House, Abercairney laid a wager with the Duke of Atholl that he could embarrass Gow, and at a suitable pause in the evening's entertainment, in front of the whole company, he demanded his reason for not repaying the loan. 'Deed, Abercairney,' Gow replied, 'if ye ha'en sense to have held your ain tongue, I would have been the last man to have spoken aboot it!'

*   *   *

You've surely heard o' the famous Niel,
The man that played the fiddle weel;
I wat he was a canty chiel,
And dearly loved the whisky, O.
And aye sin he wore tartan hose,
He dearly lo'ed the Atholl brose;
And owe was he, you may suppose,
To bid farewell to whisky, O.

184

AN EDINBURGH BUS TOUR

My wife asked me to entertain two of our grandsons who had come to stay, so I decided to take them on the top deck of an open double-decker for a sight-seeing tour of Edinburgh. (When asked later by their grandmother if they had enjoyed it, they replied that it had been a bit boring, 'but we pretended to as Jumpy [which is what they all call me] thought it was fun!)

The commentary was given by the driver, and as we moved down Princes Street this 'wag' announced: 'On your left is the Royal Scottish Academy. If you go in there, you have to pay, as the airtists are all alive and they have to eat. Behind is the National Gallery; that's free, as the airtists don't need bread as they're all deid!'

A THISTLE SERVICE

A memorable service was held on 2 July, 1987, in the High Kirk of St Giles, Edinburgh, at which two new Knights were installed to this ancient order of chivalry, thus bringing to four the number of Scots Guardsmen who were members. I was instrumental in arranging for them to be photographed after the ceremony, at which, as a brigadier in the Queens Body Guard for Scotland (the Royal Company of Archers), I was in command of the detachment on duty within the Kirk.

My party paraded with the Guard on Honour on the Castle esplanade, whence they marched down the hill.

'Do you mind if I fall out immediately after the service and we have left the Kirk? I can make it down the hill and I won't let you down inside, but I honestly don't think I can manage the march back up.' Thus spake one of my gallant band—a much respected and well known colonel of a Highland regiment, older than myself.

185

'But, of course,' I replied. What worries me, though, is what you will do when you fall out? I mean, where will you go with all your kit, clutching your bow etc.?'

'There's no need to worry at all. Within two minutes you will see me with a gin and tonic in my hand!'

The gallant colonel falls out after the Thistle service for his gin and tonic.
Photo: Professor Cheetham collection

All went well during the service, and I thought that we had acquitted ourselves with dignity. I had in fact forgotten all about the Colonel, and was standing with my detachment outside the Kirk when suddenly I heard a shout. I looked up. There, lo and behold, in a window of an apartment overlooking the serried ranks of the Royal Company, who were about to move off, was the Colonel—and in his hand a glass! He was in his daughter's flat!

I subsequently wrote a letter of congratulations to one of the newly installed Knights—Captain Sir Iain Tennant—in the Alex–Monty vein that we had once used before. His reply was as follows:

Four Scots Guards Knights of the Most Ancient and Most Noble Order of the Thistle in the Signet Library after the installation of the Earl of Airlie and Sir Iain Tennant in St Giles Cathedral, Edinburgh, on 2 July, 1987. *Left to right*: The Earl of Airlie, the Earl of Elgin and Kincardine, who bore the Sword of State, the Lord Maclean and Sir Iain Tennant.

GHQ Morayshire

SECRET

Dear Monty,

Very many thanks for your signal of comment on the four admirable young officers now elevated to the rank of the Thistle.

I remember with humility your suggestion that they should be photographed together for posterity, and I am sure that all ranks of the Base Workshops and Command Static Laundry will burst into floods of emotional salt-water tears as soon as they see those faces on the back of the *Guards Magazine*.

May I say, in passing, how very impressed we all were with the admirable bearing of the Line Regiment Archers within the Great Church. Their turn-out bore the mark of their Commander, who was put in charge. You must send me his name sometime so that I can recommend he be transferred from your Army to mine.

All the best,
sincerely,
Alex

A VISIT TO A BREWERY

A friend of mine, the chairman of a well-known brewery in Edinburgh, once insisted on my visiting the fast-canning department, of which he was very proud. I watched a woman who was sitting gazing at the cans as they moved rapidly past her, occasionally flicking a faulty one off the production line. I asked her how long she has been thus

employed, and she said since the very first day the place
was in operation. Horrified that her life was so dull, I
shouted at her, 'Do you know what I'd do if I were in charge
here?

'And what's thaat?' she shouted back.

'Every now and then I'd take you off here and put you on
another job in order to bring a little sunshine into your life.'

Without looking up she replied, to my great disappointment, 'I'll tell yu, mister, if yu did thaat, I'd have the
whole bluidy lot oot on strike in one minute flaat!'

A POSTAL INVITATION

The Scottish Postal Board decided, most kindly, to invite all
past and present General Officers commanding the Army in
Scotland to a dinner, 'to mark the long and close association
between the two organisations'. Those concerned were
asked to contact a private secretary at Postal HQ to arrange
travel and other administrative details. When I spoke to her
on the telephone from London she said, in a Morningside
accent, 'Maye word! Listening to all you generals trying to
make up your minds, aye think it a miracle that we won the
last war!'

A FIELD MARSHAL AND A MUSEUM

When I was commanding the Army in Scotland, I invited a
field marshal (and his wife) to stay and to take the salute at
the Edinburgh Tattoo. On arrival, he told me that he had
been touring Scotland and had taken the opportunity of
visiting the headquarters of some of the Scottish regiments.
He was particularly interested in, and knowledgeable about,

military museums, and as a result had visited a number in my Command.

'Very poor security in some of them,' he remarked.

'I'm sorry about that. Anything special?'

'Well, I'll give you an example: I saw in one a very valuable case of medals on the wall. It was badly fixed, so do you know what I did? When no one was looking, I turned my back on it, lifted it off the wall and hid it under my coat tails!'

'Where is it now?' I inquired, picturing a worried curator, courts of inquiry and so on.

'It was, I admit, a little embarrassing,' he replied. 'As I was saying goodbye to the Regimental Secretary and his staff, I dropped it!'

HRH Prince Edward, with Field Marshal Sir Gerald Templer who 'visited the museum', at Gogar Bank House, Edinburgh, home of the GOC, the morning after the Field Marshal had taken the salute at the Tattoo.

19
Vicissitudes of an Author

A friend of mine, a Guards General, who reached a very lofty position in the Army, decided that on retirement he would become an author. His first book was fiction. When he had submitted his manuscript to his publishers, so I was told, he was asked to call on them. He was informed: 'Rightly or wrongly, modern novels have to contain a certain amount of sex and violence, you know.'

'Oh dear,' he said, 'haven't I put in enough?'

'That's just the trouble,' came the reply. 'You've put in too much!'

One of his daughters commented, apparently: 'Wherever did he learn about all that?'

I have not myself ventured into fiction but, curiously, my wife says that I should!

BOOK-SIGNING SESSIONS

The first time it was suggested that I should try to promote sales of one of my books by signing sessions, I consulted my brother-in-law, Brough Scott. His comment was: 'Very dodgy. When once I did it, there I sat, and no one came up with my book to ask me to sign it until at last one woman did. 'But that's not my book,' I told her. '*That's* my book there.' Whereupon she retorted, "Oh I don't want *that* trash!"'

Sales promotion at Horse Guards. Two of my grandsons rally round for a good cause!

From my limited experience, I would agree that it's a risky business. A possible solution might be to enlist the help of the most attractive female members of my family to draw the potential customers in. (The corollary of this, in a different context, is when I am invited to buy a flag by a can-rattling lady cash-seeker, active in a cause that does not particularly interest me. Sometimes I say, 'Sorry, I only buy from the *plain* girls.' The effect is most interesting!)

A TALE OF A LITERARY LUNCH

I was told that 'literary lunches' were good for promotion, but I had never attended one in any capacity. This particular one happened to be held in the delightful town of Buxton. The organisers were charming, the meal excellent, and those who attended were clearly interested in literature— otherwise, I assumed, they would not be there. I was in a group of three authors, and after lunch each in turn rose and spoke about his or her book. One had written about psychic matters and spoke rather longer than the other two of us. She was, however, quite clever in her approach, announcing that when any luncher came up to buy her book—which, like us, she would sign—she would tell each, with the help of her psychic skills, what the future held in store! As a result, a large queue formed up for *her*, while *we* had only a handful.

I had been told that after lunch I would be taken some distance by car to where I could catch the train to London (missing it would entail a wait of several hours). I was, however, to have a fellow-traveller—the psychic author. I lingered as the minutes ticked by, and she was still signing her book and foretelling futures! The longer I waited, the more anxious I became, but at last she wandered out and joined me.

'For goodness' sake,' I told the driver, 'step on the gas. We're dead pushed to catch this train.' Off we set—and fast. When we arrived, there was the train, actually in the station! I jumped out, hastening my fellow-traveller, who was a slow mover, on to the platform. We made it by the skin of our teeth. A nervous wreck, I sank down in the carriage as we moved off, exhausted and breathless. 'That was lucky,' I gasped.

'Why were you so worried?' my colleague asked.

'Well, we only just caught the train, that's why!'

'Oh, *I* wasn't worried. Being psychic, I *knew* we were going to be all right.'

SALES

I couldn't understand why, as far as I could see, there were no copies of my book in the Edinburgh shops. Indeed, many of my friends had told me how difficult they found it to get a copy of *Jottings in a General's Notebook*. I decided that action was necessary, so four times a day for four days I rang up the principal bookshops, using each time a different voice, tone and accent. On the fifth day, I went to one of these shops and asked, 'Have you got a book in—I think it's called something like *'Notes in a Corporal's Exercise Book?'*

'My word,' replied the girl behind the counter, 'you've got the name wrong, but I know exactly the one you mean. The telephone has never stopped ringing with people asking about it. It is fantastically popular!'

This reminds me of the ruse of imitation in a different context. Lady Desborough was a great Edwardian hostess and lived in state at Taplow Court. She once asked her butler to despatch on her behalf a telegram, accepting an invitation. Familiar with the effusive style of his mistress, he wrote: 'Yes. How perfectly wonderful. Love, love, love'.

The invitation had, in fact, come from a senior official of the Thames Conservancy Board!

A RADIO INTERVIEW

One of the features of radio interviews, apparently, is that you are never told what is going to happen—and that goes for TV too—as spontaneity is the thing. Thus it was that on one occasion I found myself in Broadcasting House to promote one of my books and to take part in what my family told me was a *very* well-known programme, or 'chat show'. (They assured me that the interviewer was famous. 'She's much more important than you ever were!')

Anyhow, I was ushered into a studio along with a jazz pianist, a well-known personality in the world of books and journalism, a man whose hobby was collecting advertisements, and a motherly figure whom I recalled from the past as a glamour-girl who had featured large in a scandal that had nearly toppled the government of the day. It was *she* who, when asked during the programme what her current interests were, looked at me and said that she was 'deep into military research.'

The conversation was skilfully conducted by our hostess, who was a past master at it all. Informality had already been impressed on us. 'Now,' she said, 'we don't often have a general on this programme, even a retired one.' And suddenly turning to me, she asked, 'I suppose that your military training has left a mark on you that lasts for ever?'

'Like what?' I replied.

'Well, what about clean shoes?' I should think that you're pretty hot on them?'

I suppose in principle she must have been right, but it was some time since I'd actually had to buff them up myself. My answer was that I was very keen on punctuality, and that as a result I quite often caught the train before the one that I had intended, for fear of being late.

As I said this, I felt that I had left an unfavourable impression not only on my fellow-participants but, more importantly, on the thousands who, I was told, were listening in. Had I left them all with a false picture of the British General? At any rate, it cannot have been quite as misleading as the impression gained by the shop assistant in a large store, when the wife of a retired officer in the Navy, whose appointment required him to wear court dress, came into his department. 'I want to buy a pair of black silk stockings for my husband,' she said, to which the assistant replied, 'Oh, I am *so* sorry, madam.'

Postscript

In this book I have tried to touch on the amusing and bizarre things in Life. I close, however, on a more serious note, and write about three scholars of Winchester College who were all my contemporaries.

The first was Frank Thompson, son of Edward Thompson, poet and Indian historian. He had a working knowledge of nine European languages and was commissioned into the Royal Artillery in 1940. The second was David Scott-Malden, who joined the RAF at the outbreak of war, serving in Fighter Command, and was awarded the DSO, DFC and bar and the Norwegian war cross.

Frank Thompson.

Frank wrote a poem, dated 9 December, 1939, dedicated to his friend, David:

Together, my friend,
We smiled at death in the evening,
Recalling the goodness of grey stones and laughter;
Knowing how little either of us mattered,
We found a kind of happiness, if not peace.

You went, my friend,
To spread your wings on the morning;
I to the gun's cold elegance; and one
—Did you too feel the passing of a shadow
Between the glasses?—one will not return.

It was prophetic: Frank did not return. He was parachuted into Yugoslavia and, with a group of Bulgarian partisans, was ambushed near Sofia. He was treated as a rebel and 'tried' at Litakovo, defending himself in fluent Bulgarian and condemning Fascism. He was shot on 31 May, 1944.

The third scholar was the wittiest man I ever knew, and after a year up at Christ Church, Oxford, he was commissioned into the Royal Artillery. He kept wicket for the Winchester 1st eleven and wrote this poem for 'Fallen Oxford Sportsmen':

Sometimes it will come to us
Pausing beneath the fan-vaulting of the staircase,
Or in a sudden shadow trailing
Over the brittle pool and aslant the corners
Of ancient buildings.

Sometimes it will come to us
Under the fitting shadow of decline,
When there is sunlight dying on grey stone
And darkness on the lawn below lighted windows
One Oxford evening.

Roddy Gow.

Or it may come to us quickly
In joy of summer, in white figures moving
Far over hazy grass, in the run towards the wicket,
Clopping of ball on bat, brain, eye and hand consenting
June days in Sussex.

Often it will come to us
Where we have known you—in the great quadrangle,
Upland and field and moor, and we shall honour
Action and strength, for you were strong and are still,
Whom England honours.

This scholar and sportsman was my only brother, Roddy,
who was killed in action at Arnhem with the 1st Airborne
Division on 18 September, 1944. He lies buried with his

British and Polish comrades in the beautiful cemetery at Oosterbeek. He had been posted as 'missing believed prisoner of war', but on my twenty-first birthday I found him there.

David, the survivor of the three, wrote this in his memory:

> They surely smile, the stars that nightly look
> Upon your resting place; as we would smile
> Who shared the richness of your life awhile,
> And knew the laughter of the ways you took,—
> They surely smile, and through the autumn smoke
> Shine red to warm you in the midnight hours,
> As you lie blanketed by Flemish flowers,
> The sky your ceiling, and the turf your cloak.
> Then, when the sunlight on the eastern hill
> Drives them to seek their refuge in the sea,
> They pause reluctant in the dawn, until
> In grief their countenance is veiled: as we
> May pause, and turn our faces, and be still,
> For sorrow not to bear you company.

David
Scott-Malden

On his headstone, at the suggestion of his mother and friends, are these words of Achilles from Homer's *Iliad*, written in Greek, a translation of which reads:

> If I remain here, I shall not see my homeland again, but I shall enjoy immortal renown.

Reflect on these things.